THE SUFI MESSAGE

INDEX TO

VOLUMES I to XIII

THE SUFI MESSAGE

The complete set contains the following 14 volumes:

I
The Way of Illumination

II
The Mysticism of Music, Sound and Word

III
The Art of Personality

IV
Mental Purification and Healing

V
Spiritual Liberty

VI
The Alchemy of Happiness

VII
In an Eastern Rose Garden

VIII
Sufi Teachings

IX
The Unity of Religious Ideals

X
Sufi Mysticism

XI
Philosophy, Psychology, Mysticism

XII
The Divinity of the Human Soul

XIII
Sacred Readings: The Gathas

XIV
Index to Volumes I-XIII

Pir-o-Murshid
Hazrat Inayat Khan

INDEX TO
VOLUMES I to XIII

Hazrat Inayat Khan

MOTILAL BANARSIDASS PUBLISHERS PVT. LTD.
DELHI

First Indian Edition: 1990

Also available at
MOTILAL BANARSIDASS
Chowk, Varanasi 221 001
Ashok Rajpath, Patna 800 004
24 Race Course Road, Bangalore 560 001
Bungalow Road, Jawahar Nagar, Delhi-110 007
120 Royapettah High Road, Mylapore, Madras 600 004

Vol. Index ISBN: 81-208-0777-4 (Cloth)
ISBN: 81-208-0785-5 (Paper)
Set ISBN: 81-208-0494-5 (Cloth)
ISBN: 81-208-0495-3 (Paper)

PRINTED IN INDIA
BY JAINENDRA PRAKASH JAIN AT SHRI JAINENDRA PRESS, A-45 NARAINA INDUSTRIAL AREA, PHASE I, NEW DELHI 110028 AND PUBLISHED BY NARENDRA PRAKASH JAIN FOR MOTILAL BANARSIDASS PUBLISHERS PVT. LTD., BUNGALOW ROAD, JAWAHAR NAGAR, DELHI 110007.

PREFACE TO THE SERIES

THE present volume is the first of a series including all the works intended for publication of Hazrat Inayat Khan (Baroda 1882–New Delhi 1927), the great Sufi mystic who came to the Western world in 1910 and lectured and taught there until his passing away in 1927.

A new edition of this series, which was published for the International Headquarters of the Sufi Movement in the West in the '60s, is now made available in the Indian subcontinent and the Middle East. In this way Hazrat Inayat Khan's inspired and universal vision of the Sufi Message returns to his own beloved country, where it originated and where interest in it is growing.

This book and other volumes of this series have not been written down by the author. They contain his lectures, discourses and other teachings as taken down in shorthand and other handwriting. When preparing for publication great care was taken, not only to avoid distortion of their intent and meaning, but also to leave intact, as far as possible, the flow of mystical inspiration and poetical expression which add so much to their spell, and without which a significant part of his message would be lost. Although speaking in a tongue foreign to him, he moulded it into a perfect vehicle for his thought, at times somewhat ungrammatical and unusual, but always as clear and precise as his often difficult and abstruse subjects would allow.

It goes without saying that neither in the present nor in the previous edition anything has been altered which would involve even the slightest deviation from the author's intention and no attempt has been made to transform his highly personal and colourful language into idiomatically unimpeachable English. Already so much is necessarily lost by the transfer of the spoken word to the printed page, that every effort has been made, as it should, to preserve the Master's melodious phrasing, the radiance of his personality, and the subtle sense of humour which never left him.

Hazrat Inayat Khan's teaching was nearly all given during the years 1918–1926. It covers a great many subjects, several of which were grouped in series of lectures and taken up again some years later. Certain

subjects may cover nearly the same ground as others; stories and examples which abound in most of his works are met again elsewhere; and much of what he taught one finds repeated in several places. This was intentional, as repetition belonged to Hazrat Inayat Khan's method of teaching; it is for the student to become aware of the subtle differences in each context. For these and other reasons it would be difficult to follow a rigid system in publishing Hazrat Inayat Khan's works; a chronological grouping of his lectures would be very unsatisfactory, and a stringent classification according to subject-matter hardly feasible.

The complete series contains fourteen volumes. The last volume is the Index. This edition is the first one to present an index to the Sufi Message of Hazrat Inayat Khan.

Each volume is complete in itself, and therefore may be read without any necessity to study following or previous ones. However, one may get a spiritual and mental appetite to continue reading. One will find that a meditative way of reading will convey not only the words but also the spiritual power emanating from them, tuning mind, heart and soul to the pitch which is one's own.

W.v.L.

PREFACE TO INDEX VOLUME

This General Index of *The Sufi Message of Hazrat Inayat Khan* has been prepared, at the suggestion of the publisher, for inclusion in the historic Indian edition of 1988-90. The first twelve volumes of the series were originally published from 1960 to 1967, and the thirteenth volume was added in 1982. None of these volumes contained an index, but the difficulty of locating material in so many volumes has led to several informal indices over the years; for example, serveral lists of chapter headings have appeared in various countries. This is, however, the first attempt at making an inclusive and detailed index.

Naturally, such a large undertaking could not be done in a reasonable time by one person, and so a team of indexers worked through the various volumes (see Acknowledgements). No doubt this results in some inconsistency, since no two people would ever index a book the same way. However, all the indexers worked with the same general instructions, and certain key words, such as God, message, and soul, were noted especially. Whenever possible, a contextual phrase is given for words with multiple entries. Chapter titles and sub-headings are included, but are indexed like any other entry; thus, for example, "The Gift of Eloquence" will be found under "Eloquence, gift of", and "The Religion of the Heart" will be found under both "Religion" and "Heart". It should be noted that some of the material in the Volumes, particularly Volume V, is not the actual writing of Hazrat Inayat Khan, but a presentation of his teachings by his followers, Sherifa Goodenough and Mary Zohra Williams. However, since these are included in the Volumes, they are included in the Index as well.

The intention has been to make the index inclusive, so when there was doubt about an entry our inclination was to put it in. There must remain many errors of omission and some of commission, but our hope is that this index will prove useful to the many readers throughout the world who find inspiration and guidance in the teachings of Hazrat Inayat Khan.

ACKNOWLEDGEMENTS

The enormous amount of detail work to produce this Index has been undertaken by a team of willing volunteers. Sharif Graham was responsible for the overall co-ordination of the project, with abundant assistance from Aziza Salvato. Individual volumes were indexed by Murshida Vera Corda, Rabia Longworth, Telema Hess, Munir and Ruhia Nienhaus, Arabella Droullard, Gary Hal Anderson, Khusrau Bob Carrel, Evelyn Boatright, Aziza Salvato and Sharif Graham. In addition, Hal Anderson, Munir Nienhaus, Aziza Salvato and Sharif Graham each did a second volume. The final process of computer entry was assisted by a grant from the Hazrat Inayat Khan Memorial Trust.

Aab
I.112
V.26
Abandonment
I.56
Abda
XII.133
Abdullah
XII.141
Ab-e Hayat
IV.81
Abi Ruh
XIII.233
Ablutions
IX.197
inner and outer -, XIII.212-13, 216-17
Abnormal
IX.255
Abode, eternal
I.170
IX.37
Abraham
I.33
II.202
V.210
VII.24, 79
IX.147, 150, 170-2, 186, 193, 198, 208, 210, 218-9, 236, 252, 270
X.154
XII.133
XIII.126
Abrams, Dr.
II.107
XI.28
Absolute
I.111
VIII.153
IX.101
Abstinence
XIII.31, 183-4
Abu Hashim Madani, Murshid
II.233, 244
IV.156, 264
VII.259
VIII.231, 284
IX.115
XI.214
XII.105, 148-50, 163
XIII.150
"There is only one virtue...", IX.115
Abu Bakr
XII.103
Abul Ala
V.18
Abu Said
XII.157
Abuse
sexual - of children, III.184-6
Accident
IV.122, 211, 227
V.95
VII.57
XI.211
warning of -s, IV.254
Accommodation
VIII.130
X.197
XI.54, 238
Accomplishment
I.58,66
IX.48, 132
XII.77
Acknowledgment
VI.263-7
Acquaintances
dealing with -, III.247-8
Acting
I.78-9
Action
I.68
II.29, 237, 240
V.94
VI.233
VII.150
VIII.151-2
IX.15, 178, 273, 277
X.51-5, 151
XI.49, 119, 196
freedom of -, I.82
the law of -, V.30-1; VI.233-9

three stages of -, IX.245
Activity
I.67-9
IV.89
VII.39
IX.100
X.247
XI.63
Actor
I.78
IX.205
XI.147-8
Adab
XIII.193-7
Adam
I.140
II.34, 52
III.34, 124, 165
V.35, 113, 231, 233
VI.30
VII.180
VIII.13, 155, 214, 256
IX.230
XI.250
XIII.122
- and Eve, II.66; III.161
Adaptability
IX.256
Addiction
IX.209
Adept
XI.166, 168
meditation of -, XI.168
Adharma
III.227
Adhikar
V.125
Adjustment
VIII.321
Admiration
III.262
Adoration
IX.48
Adultery
III.129-30
Advaita
IX.257
Advanced
spiritually -, IX.115
Advancement
VI.226
IX.50
spiritual -, XI.237
Advice
VII.83
Adviser
VII.83
Aetsh
I.112
Affection
VII.73
XI.188
Affinity
II.38
- between positive and negative, III.127
Aftab
V.25
Age(s)
IV.113
VI.115
IX.165
copper -, I.221; X,223
golden -, I.220, VIII.214; X.201, 223; XIII.183
iron -, VIII.214; X.223-4; XIII.183
silver -, I.220-1; X.223
Agitation
X.266-7
Agra
IV.156
X.204
Ahad
V.17
Ahadiat
I.111
V.25, 33
Ahankar
XIII.184
Ahriman
VIII.19
IX.178
Ahura Mazda
II.65
VIII.19

IX.176, 178
Aim
VIII.24-7
IX.52
- of creation, IX.181
- of soul, VII.181
- of Sufi, VIII.24
man's - in life, XII.76-8
'Aina Khana
I.149
IV.241
Ain al-Iman
I.55-6
Air
I.112
IX.219
element, X.161
sound of -, II.15
Ajanta
X.193
Ajmer
II.60, 203
XII.140
Ajnana
VI.27
Ajsam
I.111
V.25
Akasha(s)
I.1XII.220140, 147-9, 151-6
II.97, 125
IV.134
VI.233
IX.220, 273
X.197
XI.24, 30
Akbar
II.137
III.180
X.224-5, 228
XIII.77
Akhlak(-e) Allah
IV.277
IX.111, 120, 144
X.69
XII.17
XIII.193
Akhlak(-e) Jalali
XII.136
Aladdin
III.173
IV.215
V.201
VI.69
VII.36
IX.183
XII.26, 82
Alam
II.66
Alam-e-Mithal
VIII.182
Alchemy
I.152
II.99
IV.203
V.216
VI.11-3
IX.118
XI.53
XII.48
- of happiness, V.216-7; VI.7ff; XII.88
Algosa
II.57
Alhamdolillah
XII.160
Al haya wal iman

Ali
I.27
V.21, 205
VIII.14, 179
IX.199, 223, 240
X.101-2
XII.91, 103
XIII.93, 157
- on fear, VII.229
"I believe in God...", IX.224
"Is there really...?", I.177
"Know thyself...", I.20; IX.240; XIII.172
Alias, Saint
XIII.38
Ali Baba
- and the Forty Theives, XII.123

Alif
I.40
II.66
Ali Khan, Mohammad
XII.154
Alim
II.66
XIII.100
Alima
V.26
XII.34
All
V.78
the word -, II.66
Allah
I.41, 46
II.36, 66
V.14, 203
IX.171, 258
XI.201
akhlak-e -, IX.111
- and ideal, V.187
--ho-Akbar, XII.160
Allahabad
II.205
Allah Hu
II.66
Alleluia
XII.122
All-Good
God as -, IX.178
All-wise
IX.125
Almighty
I.214
IX.108, 155
Alpha
VI.186
XI.167
XIII.125
- and Omega, IX.16-17, 31, 136, 181, 183, 228, 238-9, 247, 277
Alphabet
II.35
IX.37
Altar
IX.272
Aluk
II.64
IX.37
Amazement
X.137
Ambition
VI.203
Ameen
II.66
IX.37
Amen
II.66
IX.37
America
IX.167
X.229
XII.151
Amin
III.223
IX.194
- *the Faithful Trustee* (play), XII.233-74
Amir
III.191
IV.259
V.163, 247
VII.69
VIII.121
X.125
XIII.237
"He who has lost...", I.21; IX.49
Amir Minai
V.236
Ammara
V.25
XI.202
XII.34
XIII.181
Amr-e Allah
V.61, 83
Anahad
II.63
Analysis
IV.233
XI.74
inadequate -, VII.100
light of -, IX.165-6

Ananda
VI.28
Anandamayakosh
IX.219, 221
XIII.127
Ancestry
- of religions, IX.176
Ancient Places
II.209
Andar (Antar)
V.162
Angel(s)
I.98, 115, 117, 119-22, 133
II.18, 52, 79
V.100, 102, 113, 193
VII.115, 240
VIII.119, 275
IX.86
X.87
XI.241, 251
-ic accomplishment, I.182-3
-ic heavens, I.122, 137-9; XI.249
-ic qualities, I.91, 117, 136-7
-ic quality, XI.155, 157
-ic souls, XI.240
-ic sphere(s), VI.226; VII.240; XI.241
-ic world, XI.154
- Man, I.98-101
- symbolize breath, XIII.139
communication with -, I.118-21
five principle -s, V.103
guardian -, I.119
Jacob wrestling with -, V.100-4
world of -, I.179-83
Anger
II.143
VII.142
XI.229
XII.91
Animal(s)
II.210, 248
V.71
VII.69
VIII.28
IX.101-2, 118, 184, 225
X.26, 189-90
XI.63, 114, 236
- kingdom, I.28, 90, 111, II.13, 179, 186
- quality, XI.155
- worship, IX.76
killing of -, IX.201
knowledge of -s, VII.148
Annamayakosh
XIII.127
Annihilation
I.21-2, 39, 184
II.249-50, 262
VI.277
VIII.180, 187
IX.172, 174, 218
X.134
XI.248
Ansar
V.85, 246
Answer
XI.227
- as echo, VIII.130
- to every question, IX.82
Antipathy
XIII.238
Anuwadi
II.54
Anvar
V.85, 246
Anxiety
VIII.51
Aphorisms
- (book), XI.225-59
Apostles
VI.131, 154
IX.245
twelve -, IX.228; X.189
Appearance(s)
I.80
V.119
IX.18, 80-1
XI.152
Appendicitis
IV.33
Appetite(s)
VI.191
bodily -, XIII.182, 187
five - of man, VI.17-8

Appreciation
I.218
IX.42
XI.241
Apuleius
XIII.30
Aqibat
-, *Life after Death* (book), V.37-78
Arabia
IX.148, 252
X.204, 221, 253
Arabian
X.203-4
- *Nights*, VI.12; VIII.14, 227
Arabic
X.215
Arabs
X.215, 256
XIII.16
Architecture
X.196-206
Ardhangi
III.121
V.35
Arguments
VII.257
XI.246
Aristocracy
III.113
VI.53
VII.173
VIII.239
IX.30, 96, 120, 126-7
X.91, 244-5
XII.35
- of religion, IX.120-1
Aristotle
VIII.22
Arjuna
V.198
IX.162, 241
XIII.28
Arsh
I.116
V.28
Art
I.143
II. 80, 96, 138, 190, 216
III.183, 214
VI.44, 110
IX.48-9, 90, 196
X.159, 163, 165-6, 168-71, 175-8, 180, 184, 186-8, 190, 192-4
XI.139, 147, 192-3
- and nature, XII.33
- and religion, X.168-71
- of personality, III.214-28; VI.44-51
-: *Yesterday, To-day and Tomorrow* (book), X.155ff
divine -, XI.256
divinity of -, X.163-7
essence of -, X.159-62
ideal of -, X.175-9
influence of works of -, II.216
Artha
VII.206
IX.259
Artificiality
I.147-8
Artist
I.143-4
II.260
IX.175
X.259
XI.166-7, 193
- as God, VIII.109
Arwah
I.111
V.25
Aryans
IX.156, 176
Asana
VI.101
Asceticism
I.207-8
X.87
Ascetic(s)
IV.129
VIII.74
IX.90, 257
Ashik
XII.161
Ashraf al Makhluqat

I.27
V.11-2, 104
Ashtapadis
III.172
Asiatic
X.215
Asif of Hyderabad
VII.137
VIII.142
XIII.236
Asman(s)
I.111-2, 140, 152
Aspirations
VIII.272
human -, IX.83-4
Assam
X.203
Assertion
VII.191
Assimilation
VIII.158
XI.42-3, 49
- of the message, IX.245-6
manifestation, gravitation, - and perfection, VIII.153-62
Associate(s)
II.211
Association
II.210
Astrology
II.90, 99, 174, 189
III.26
IV.46, 254
V.98
XI.171
XIII.46
Astronomers
XI.54
Astronomy
II.189
Asura
I.179
Asylums
IV.37
Atesh
V.26
Atma
I.160
IV.184
V.83, 87
VIII.28
Atman
IV.189, 197
VI.11
Atmosphere
II.20, 82, 132, 201, 205, 209, 221
IV.133, 156
XI.14, 34-7, 85
XII.105
XIII.82, 164
Atoms
IV.82
V.102
X.42
physical and mental -, IV.65
At-one-ment
VIII.274
IX.35, 123, 196
XII.112
Attachment
I.208
II.28, 228
III.154, 262
V.43
VI.123-4
X.136
Attainment
I.23, 93
III.257
V.201, 214
VI.195, 201-5
VII.45, 139, 229
IX.83, 87, 108, 259, 266
X.97
XI.168, 235
- of inner life, I.93-7
higher -. V.201-3
life's -, secret of, IX.52
material -, IX.174
path of -, VI.195-206
spiritual -, I.221; VI.17, 41, 195; VII.232; IX.87, 132, 174, 215; XI.235, 244
Attar
(see Farid-ud-Din Attar)

Attitude
I.52
II.82, 102
III.72, 205
IV.41, 47, 100, 151, 219
VI.60-7, 261
VIII.114-17, 224-6, 247-8
IX.115
X.35, 110, 131
XI.99-102, 127, 234
XIII.268-9
- of a disciple, X.110-14
control over -, XI.99
friendly -, III.227
hopeful -, IV.48
prayerful -, V.204-6
right -, VI.63
Sufi -, IX.114
two -s toward life, III.205-6
Attraction
I.98
III.121
V.89
VI.62, 129
XI.103, 105, 112-3
- and repulsion, III.123-5; XII.39
- of blood, VIII.91
- of occupation, VIII.93
- of opposities, VIII.94-5
- of qualities, VIII.93
- to God, IX.35
law of -, III.121; VIII.91-6
Attributes
VII.112
IX.84, 195, 208-9
Attunement
II.20, 82, 84, 98, 101, 137, 139, 147
Aura
I.116, 153
XI.36-7
XIII.160
Aurangzeb
I.83
V.198
Authority
IX.55
XII.43
religious -, IX.121
Autosuggestion
II.173
Aurangabad
X.193
Autocracy
VII.170
Avatar(s)
I.30-1, 33
IV.284
IX.117-8, 147, 214, 257, 257
Avicenna
IV.35, 43
X.13, 253
XII.82
Awakening
II.87, 109, 147
VII.36
VIII.302-22
IX.142, 147
XII.66
- and sleep, VII.35-6
- of soul, VII.195-7
stages of -, III.142
Awatads
I.30
Ayaz
XI.82
Ayesha
II.46
Azal
I.181
Azar
X.188
Azazil
V.103
Azrael
V.44

Baad
I.112
V.25
Baba
XII.73
Babel

tower of -, IV.168
Babies
- in kindergarten, III.34
blame of -, III.46
consciousness of higher spheres in -, III.35
controlling activity of -, III.35
definition of -, III.34
ghost stories and -, III.40
good tendencies, III.46
friend unseen for -, III.41
imitative stage in -, III.36
irritability in -, III.37
manners for -, III.44
Montessori's activities for -, III.36
moods in -, III.38
obstinancy in -, III.41-2
religion for -, III.38-9,41
rewards for -, III.43
Santa Claus and -, III.40
Baby
education of the -, III.34-52
Backwards
going -, X.107
Badishah
story of -, V.50, 57
Badness
VI.170
IX.178
Baha-ud-Din Naqshband
V.22
Balakush
IV.219
Balance
I.66, 97, 145, 147, 151
II.29, 35, 42, 48
III.16, 80
IV.17, 28, 57-8, 62, 127, 237
V.212-13
VI.85, 107, 158, 202
VIII.61-7
IX.164, 197
X.122
XI.102, 177, 255
XIII.66, 175, 190
- and meditation, VIII.65
- as chief aim, VIII.67
- as control, VIII.64
- as keynote, VIII.135
- as movement, VIII.65
- as security of life, VIII.67
- between activity and repose, IV.28
- in inner self, VIII.66
- in telling truth, VIII.61
- of life, XIII.64-6
- of thought, VIII.62
- to make thoughtfulness, VIII.64
- vs. excess, VIII.63
how to achieve -, VIII.64-5
lack of -, VIII.66: XIII.170
nature of -, VIII.64-5
teaching of -, III.16, III.63
Balder
myth of -, XIII.110-111
Ballet
II.45
Baluchistan
king of -, XII.95
Balzac
V.18
Bandeh
V.203
VIII.120
IX.171
Bandeh Navaz
V.22
Banshee
XIII.32-3
Baptism
IX.188
XII.102
Baqa
I.39, 185, 205
V.18
VIII.180
Baqi-bi-Allah
V.33, 187
Baroda, India
XII.129
Basarat
V.26
VIII.196
Basir

VIII.196
XII.61
Bast
XIII.154
Battle
IX.160-1
- with ego, XIII.175
Bawa
XII.73
Bayat
I.46-53
X.51, 85
XI.121
Bayazid
IV.54
Beatitudes, the
VII.67
IX.188-90
Beauty
I.20, 23, 98, 138, 218, 222-4
II.42,73-4, 86, 147
III.90, 158-61
IV.101
VI.171, 262
VII.11, 12-3, 55, 216-7
VIII.111, 237, 240, 242
IX.49-50, 95, 109, 111, 120, 125, 129, 149, 213-4, 239, 265, 267, 278
X.169, 186, 192-5
XI.77, 115, 139, 147, 192, 194, 227-8, 232-3, 243, 253, 256
XII.15
- of character, XI.252
definition of -, VIII.57
divine -, IX.138
divine - in every person, XI.258
focusing on -, VIII.257
inner -, XI.194
love, harmony and -, VII.11ff
love of -, VII.22
sense of -, XIII.169-70
veiling and unveiling -, III.140-1
Bedil
VI.273
VII.137-8
VIII.161
Beethoven
II.136
VI.128
VIII. 329
X.120, 231, 253
XII.75
Being
I.144, 237, 240
III.127
V.99, 240
VI.119, 146, 198, 269
VIII.56, 119, 229
IX.13, 101, 121, 125-6
XI.54, 56, 243
XI.52, 69, 241, 248
art of -, VIII.56
- of God, VIII.134, IX.101
contemplation of -, IX.110
desire of -, VIII.157
divine -, I.205, 236-8, IX.38, 111, 155, 207
innermost -, IX.167
man's -, IV.71f
one -, XI.213
oneness of -, VIII.133
only -, XI.186
original -, XI.153
perfect -, IX.114, 176
personal -, V.12-14
spiritual -, IX.187
Beings
II.212
V.240, 243
illuminated -, II.165
Belief(s)
I.45, 54-7, 204-5
II.97
IV.40, 52-3, 108, 265
VI.19, 127, 209
IX.15, 18, 27, 40, 53-9, 65, 76, 80-1, 85, 120, 162, 179, 208
XI.80-4, 100, 227, 249, 258
XII.12
XIII.12-14, 243-4
- and superstition, XIII.11-2

- in God, IV.265; IX.53; XI.204
intellectual -, VIII.279
purified -, IX.57
superstitions, customs and -, XIII.11-46
Believer(s)
I.44
IX.138, 226
Bell(s)
IV.20
IX.216
- and gongs, XIII.18-9
Beloved
I.72
II.60, 73-4, 95, 231, 244
III.134
V.11, 192
VII.11
VIII.120, 161, 180, 200
IX.265, 276
X.153, 210
XI.160, 162, 243, 247
XII.75
character of the -, III.134-7
curl of -, VIII.24; XIII.108
Divine -, XIII.100, 150, 198
eyes of -, VIII.161
face of -, VIII.74
God as -, XIII.283
Benares, India
II.203
VII.36
Beneficence
I.19
IX.254
XI.180-2
XII.21
law of -, III.243-53; VI.238
moral of -, III.191
Beni Israel
VIII.18, 163
IX.147, 148, 150, 170
XIII.21
scriptures of --, IX.149
Berkeley, California
XII.153
Berlin
X.190
Bernhardt, Sarah
VIII.234
Bewilderment
I.168
VIII.223, 313-4
X.93-4, 136
Bhagavad Gita
IX.146, 161
X.69
XII.161
Bhakta
XII.161
Bhakti
XII.149
Bhakti Yoga
VII.210-1
XII.103
Bharat Khand
IX.156
Bharja
II.53
Bhartrihari
XII.130
Bhava Sagara
VI.134
VII.183
IX.222
XIII.120
Bhiksha
IX.156
Bhu-loka
I.136
Bhundara
XII.142
Bhut
VII.149
Bible
VI.30, 40, 182, 216, 259
VII.36
VIII.303, 305
IX.239
X.78, 113, 119, 122, 262, 267
XI.58, 64, 112, 150, 223, 232
XIII.25, 96, 98, 281
"Be ye perfect...", IV.114, 232
- on faith, VII.103
"God is love", VII.266

"In Him we live...", III.254; VII.45, 162
"It is the spirit...", XI.64
"Knock, and it...", VII.83
"Repent...", VII.51
"We live and move...", IV.62, IX.101, 277
"Where your treasure", VII.120, 165
Word in -, XII.119

Bigotry
III.38
IX.54

Bi-nayaz
IX.95

Bindu
XIII.99

Biology
XI.15

Bird(s)
II.26, 179
IX.225
XI.114
XIII.97
- and beasts, IV.116

Birth
I.81, 133-4, 137
VIII.160
IX.31
XI.64
- customs, India, XIII.41-2
- of God, I.137
- of man, I.137

Bismillah
XII.160

Bitra
X.212

Bitterness
III.235
IX.45-6, 229

Blame
VIII.276-9
IX.239

Blessing(s)
II.206, 222, 239
VIII.150
IX.18, 36, 107, 133, 223, 227, 246
XI.95, 241-2, 250
-, divine, IX.16
- of God, IX.227

Blindness
I.17
IX.110
XI.33

Bliss
IX.167, 260
XI.250
spiritual -, IX.225

Blood
IV.39
IX.187
XI.122

Bodhisattva
I.15
II.242
IX.130, 166, 220
XIII.128

Bodies
five - of the soul, IX.219-20
half--, III.121ff

Body
I.80, 128, 134-5, 147, 150, 166, 172, 181
II.16, 41, 47, 63, 85, 93, 107, 110, 125, 132, 144, 158, 163, 173, 232, 246, 256
IV.18, 122, 126, 129, 160, 191, 275
V.11, 84, 230-1, 235-6, 238, 240, 253
VI.152
VII.147, 194
VIII.50
IX.217
X.49
XI.20-1, 59, 68-9, 154, 196, 245
XII.14, 50
- as instrument, IV.18, 130; XIII.51, 138, 210
- as temple, VIII.50
- and mind, V.235; VIII.290
- and soul, VIII.290
- of universe, VIII.133
care of -, I.149

circulation of -, VIII.133
control of -, IV.126-31
dead -, I.194
five elements of the -, XIII.215-6
inactivity of -, VII.124
inner -, XI.146
instrument of our -, XIII.210-11
mystical significance of -, V.20
origin of -, VIII.290
perfecting of -, IV.129
physical -, I.166, 200-1, IV.127; XI.32
purity of the -, XIII.219-20
purpose of -, I.147
spiritual -, I.173
vibrations of -, XI.31

Bogey-Man
XI.223
The - (play), XII.169-94

Bohemian
- life, XIII.281

Bold
XI.135

Bombay
X.193

Book
holy -, IX.196
-s, XII.49

Bose, Jagadish Chandra
XI.61
XII.118
XIII.148

Bowing
IX.197

Boy
- and girl, III.71

Brahma
I.114, 193
VI.30, 11
VIII.38
IX.103, 108, 206, 219
XI.49, 58, 152, 217
XIII.273
-'s dream, IV.157; XII.76; XIII.70
- taking honey, XIII.247

Brahmachari
V.120

Brahmacharya-shrama
VII.209
XII.109

Brahmanism
IX.157, 164, 168

Brahmin
II.223
V.125
VIII.298, 145
IX.37, 155-6, 158, 168, 215-6, 257
X.105, 246
XII.45
-s, V.121
-s and food, IV.70
consulting -, XII.40

Brain
II.229
IV.134
V.230
XI.231
XII.17

Brama
X.188

Bread
IX.187-8

Breast
- of the Prophet, IX.228-30

Breath
I.115, 121, 123, 133, 152
II.18, 48, 55, 74, 92, 110, 114, 124, 135, 143, 158, 163, 172, 180, 203, 221
IV.17, 58. 66, 72, 74, 81, 100, 155, 190, 274
V.214, 220
VI.14
VII.102-6, 142-3
VIII.51, 206-7
IX.176, 202, 219, 230, 250
X.213
XI.197
XII.50
XIII.135-164; 211-12
Be conscious of every -, XIII.151-2

blessings in -, V.11
- and magnetism, XIII.162-3
- as prana, VIII.206
- in development of mind, XIII.153-4
- is likened to water, XIII.161
- of God, I.113-14
-, vehicle of the self, XIII.142-3
channel of the -, XIII.140-1
clear -, XIII.211
communication through -, XIII.155-7
culture of -, XIII.136-7
direction of -, XIII.152-3
divine -, I.171-7
exercises of -, I.153, IX.215-6
five aspects of -, XIII.138-40
full -, XIII.149-50
length and breadth of -, XIII.157-8
mystery of -, VII.102-9; XIII.164
mysticism of -, XIII.143-4
power of -, IV.74-5; XIII.135-6
purity of -, XIII.216-7
regularity of -, XIII.147
rhythm of -, XI.31; XIII.141-2
rhythmic -, XIII.150-1
secret of -, IV.188-94
subtle waves of -, XIII.163-4
universal -, IX.178
what power of - can do, VII.142-4

Breathing
IV.66-7, 100
- and meditation, XIII.161
healing by -, IV.81f

Bridegroom
IX.226

Brindaban
VIII.178

Brotherhood
I.18
III.100, 244
IX.13, 18, 263, 267
X.261-70
XI.183-7
- of Purity, XII.146
spirit of -, IX.20
universal -, IX.256, 268

Buddh
IX.166-7, 240

Buddha
I.15, 128
II.242
VI.27, 105, 114, 183
VII.106
VIII.118, 296
IX.86, 125, 143, 150, 164-8, 179, 233, 247, 264, 269, 271-2, 277
X.16, 67, 96, 109, 143, 154, 253-4
XI.18, 167, 199, 227
XII.43, 105
XIII.16
- on fear, VII.133
Gautama -, XII.133

Buddhism
VI.230
VIII.18-9, 119, 142, 163, 166, 265
IX.166-8, 169
X.253, 257, 262
mission of -, VIII.296

Buddhist(s)
IX.166-7, 258
X.105, 125
XI.164
XIII.19, 21
- in Burma, XII.35
- sages, XII.113, 116

Bullah Shah
I.40
V.20
VII.202

Buraq
VII.106
IX.230
XIII.121, 142

Burbank, Luther
IV.134

Burma
X.203
XII.35

Business
- dealings I.219-20
- world of Muhammad, IX.194

Bustan
X.144

Buttase
VII.91

Buzurg(i)
IX.128, 129
XIII.194

Byzantium
X.229

Caliph Vathek
XII.138

Candles
I.122
IX.244, 272

Capacity
II.123
XI.20-4, 29, 35, 39, 41, 58, 61-2

Capital
XII.54

Captivity
VII.188, 190

Caste(s)
V.125
XII.107
XIII.115
- system in Hinduism, IX.156-7

Cat
IX.201

Caterpillar
IV.266

Catholic
IX.257
XIII.17

Cause
I.87
IV.60
V.12, 199-201
- and effect, V.12; XI.25, 28
primal -, IX.48

Celibacy
III.165-9
XIII.218

Centres
II.158
IV.38, 130
VI.46
XI.21
XIII.136
intuitive -, IV.131
nervous -, XI.196

Ceremony
IX.162, 264

Chaitanya
I.113

Chakra(s)
II.158
IX.214
XIII.93

Chaldeans
X.256

Chama
XIII.28

Change
I.166-7
II.40, 177, 220
VII.40
X.110

Chaos
IX.36

Character
II.53
III.197
IV.285
VIII.234-40
XI.135-6, 177
XII.86
beauty of -, XI.252
--building, III.197-213; VIII.234-6
- and fate, VII.110-18
nature and -, XI.134-41

Charity
IX.197-8

Charm
IV.80, 92
healing by -s, IV.80

Chatura
II.45

Cheerfulness
XI.247
Chehl, Mohammad
V.66
Chela
IX.155
Cherags
IX.272
Child
IX.15, 31, 96
XI.179, 188
education of the -, III.53ff
Childhood
IX.56
XI.135, 154-5
beginning of -, III.53,55
ideals of -, III. 55-59,62
Childlike
I.89
Children
I.223
II.138, 223, 244
III.53
XI.86
anger in -, III.49
- and family, III.67-8
- knowing place, III.59
- learning customs, III.67
- learning endurance, III.63
- making stories, III.65-6
- of God, IX.140
correcting -, III.73
cultivating qualities of -, III.69,71
cycles in -'s lives, III.70-1,73-4
education of -, III.87ff
emotions of -, III.79
energetic -, III.91
freedom of -, III.100
God-ideal for -, III.65
gymnastics for -, III.69
inclinations of -, III.61
insolence of -, III.55
intellectual development of -, III.66
morals for -, III.100
movement for -, III.69
mind of -, III.68-9,94
music for -, III.70
nature of, IX.36
obedience in -, III.50
over-enthusiasm in -, III.43
perversion in -, III.184-5
play of -, III.50,95
punishing -, III.48
reasoning with -, III.47
rhythm of -, III.55,97
spirituality, guiding -
training of -, III.106, 185
spoiling -, III.81-2
soul of -, III.66
stubborn -, III.47
teaching -, III.64
work for -, III.73
China
X.179, 187-9, 193, 203, 223
art of -, X.180-2
Chinese
X.80, 223
XIII.16
- philosopher, XIII.101, 104-5
Chisti, Moin-ud-Din
(see Moin-ud-Din Chisti)
Chistia
I.41
II.60
V.32
VIII.14, 18
XIII.31
- Khandan, XII.146
- school, IV.284
Chitrani
III.136
Chivalry
III.149-52
Choice
I.138
Choudatabaq
I.39
VIII.321
Christ, Jesus
(see also Jesus Christ)
the spirit of -, IX.183-7
Christhood
IX.242
Christianity

IX.170, 188
X.253
XII.158
self-denial in -, XIII.171

Christian(s)
IX.257
X.257
XI.164
- churches, XIII.18

Christian Science
IV.39

Church
VI.47
IX.22, 64, 205, 239257
- of All, IX.274-9
foundation of -, IX.144

Circle
V.135
symbol of -, XIII.99

Circulation
IV.15
spiritual -, VIII.131

Circumstances
VII.213-4
XI.125

Civilization
III.199
VII.171, 178
VIII.78, 200
XI.232

Claim
- of prophethood, IX.138

Clairaudience
V.246
VIII.302
XII.21

Clairvoyance
II.177
V.246
VIII.302
XII.21

Clarity
IX.167

Classes
II.27
III.132
VIII.157

Cleanliness
IV.18
VI.240
IX.28
XIII.209-11
laws of -, IX.197

Cleverness
VII.230
IX.66
XI.149
XII.100

Cobra
IV.193
V.201
VII.142
IX.102, 183
XIII.139, 152-3, 160

Cock-fighting
IV.143

Colour
II.38, 63, 121, 127-8
III.28
IV.59
VIII.26
X.160-2, 183, 200
XI.29-30, 32, 45, 85
XII.39
XIII.144-5
mystery of sound and -, II.121-6
red -s, XI.85
spiritual significance of sound and -, II.127-34

Colombia University
XII.152

Columbus
IV.121

Comfort
XII.85

Commandments
ten -, IX.173

Commercialism
IX.63, 248
XII.57

Communication
II.120, 133, 175, 181, 190, 227
VIII.304-5
X.128

- with oneself, X.48-9
Communion
II.133
IV.203, 208
VI.126
VIII.293, 304
IX.99
XI.151
Communism
XII.56
Comparison
IV.101
VII.88
IX.80, 180
Compassion
I.216
VI.235
IX.55, 94
XI.177
Competition
IX.248
XI.47
XII.36
learning -, III.95-6
Complaining
III.205
VIII.285
Complaint
name of -, IV.30
Completion
IX.127
Complexities
IX.187
Complexity
IV.124
VIII.282
X.25
XI.18
- and simplicity, VII.239-44
Composer
XI.257
Comprehension
IX.103
Concealment
IX.129
Conceit
I.76
Concentration
II.20-1, 102, 126, 169, 233, 236, 238, 255, 260
IV.16, 122, 138, 152-5, 167, 236
V.33
VI.13, 111, 143, 167
VII.128-9, 140, 197
IX.115
X.26-7, 163
XI.77
XII.24, 61, 66, 77
XIII.20, 60, 146, 220
- in love, VII.78
- of infant, III.17-18
-s, XI.69
four grades of -, IV.154-6
power of -, IV.78
Conception
XI.42, 103
- of God, IX.113
Sufi -, IX.276
Conciliation
III.204
VI.52
VIII.243-5
Condition(s)
VI.75, 171
VIII.320
adverse -, X.111
bettering -, XI.175
- of a oerson, XI.93
Confessions
XII.129-63
Confidence
I.95
VI.205
VII.91
IX.102
X.100-1, 104-5
XII.63, 100
- in oneself, XII.101
Conflict
XI.65
Confusion
VII.82
XII.65
Congestion
IV.15, 22

VIII.233
XI.46
Connection
IV.125
VII.53
Conscience
I.17, 39
IV.22, 234
V.48
VIII.199-202
IX.43, 265, 267
XI.86, 230
XIII.278-80
Conscientiousness
VI.161
Consciousness
I.39, 79-80, 111, 137, 144-5, 160, 189, 232
II.23, 37, 63, 132, 226, 237
III.138, 177, 182, 196-8, 231, 239
IV.51, 109, 120, 123, 186, 196, 229
V.32, 88, 133, 215, 240
VI.193
VII.38, 139
VIII.42, 157, 169, 196-8, 315
IX.120, 247-9
X.17
XI.69, 150, 158, 250, 255
XII.50, 93
buried -, VIII.317
- of God, IX.115, 188
- of mystic, VIII.311-3
- of self, IX.115
- of soul, VIII.315-6
developing -, VIII.289-90
expanding -, VIII.252
expansion of -, IV.229-37
great -, IX.225
higher -, IX.36
manifestation of -, V.88
new -, VIII.291
raising -, XI.158-60
real -, VIII.320
universal -, I.29
Conservative
- spirit, VIII.232-3
Consideration
III.93, 219, 223-4
VIII.142, 237-8, 322
X.99-100
XI.110
XIII.198, 264
teaching -, III.93-4
Consoler
VI.260
Consonants
- and vowels, XII.120
Constancy
III.170-1
VI.13
VIII.78
X.105
Constitution
our -, V.229-39
our physical -, V.229
Construction
XI.63
- and destruction, V.60
Contact
IV.103
Contemplation
II.169
IV.155, 171
VII.197
IX.114, 246
X.27, 77-8, 121-2
XII.24
- of perfect being, IX.110
Contentment
VII.48
IX.111
XI.101, 162
disadvantageous -, XI.101
Continence
XIII.218
Continuity
II.220
VI.272
Contraction
I.113
- and expansion, XIII.154-4
Contradiction
IX.151
XI.237

Contrast
I.24
VIII.311
Control
III.147, 199-201
IV.132
VII.112
VIII.50
XII.91
- of body, IV.126-31; VIII.49-53
- of mind, IV.132-47; VII.63; VIII.51
parental -, III.147
physical -, VIII.49-53
self--, IV.71
Convention
VIII.199-200
Conventionality
VIII.199
XI.232
XIII.280-4
Conviction
I.183, 203-4
VI.211
VII.230
VIII.270
IX.27, 57-9, 223
XIII.12
Cook
II.112
Copper Age
I.221
X.223
Corinthian
X.205
Corruption
IX.32
Cosmic
- *Language* (book), II.189-262
Cosmos
IX.125, 185, 214
XI.160
Coué, Dr.
IV.171
Counsel
IX.140
Courage
I.225
II.28
IX.106
XII.93
Courtesy
XIII.26
Courtship
III.144-8
real -, III.144
Cow
-worship (Hindu), IX.76-7
Creating
I.156
Creation
I.24, 113, 135, 157
II.14, 76, 85, 88, 123, 157, 159, 181, 185, 216, 221, 233, 237, 260
III.164
IV.151, 157
V.96
VI.30, 145
VII.35, 145-6
VIII.154, 157
IX.92-3, 107, 110, 126, 175, 183, 202, 223, 262
X.149, 195
XI.154, 158
XII.77
aim of -, IX.181
lower -, XI.67-8, 170
mental -, VII.132-8
purpose of -, VII.11; IX.192
source and goal of -, XI.256
ways of -, V.89
Creative
IX.125
- and responsive, V.95
- power, IV.257; V.95; VII.132; XII.70
Creativity
XI.108
Creator
I.237
VII.126-7
IX.92-3, 108, 175, 219
X.159, 187
- God, II.39, 42

Crescent
IX.20, 131, 268
XII.98
Crime
VI.243
- is natural, III.191
Criticism
II.228
VI.68
XI.100
Cross
I.143
IV.235
VIII.184-90
IX.174, 177, 182, 190-1, 215, 223-4, 242
meaning of symbol of -, IX.190-1
symbol of -, VIII.184-90; IX.145, 190-1, 223-5; XIII.93-5
Crowd
XI.78
Crown
- of thorns, IX.222-3
Crucifixion
III.148
IV.161
VI.205
VIII.187
IX.182, 224-5, 227, 237, 242
Cry
IX.228
answer to -, IX.243
- of humanity, IX.269
Crystal
I.91
Culture
XII.34
highest aspect of -, XI.232
Moral - (book), III.229-62
Cupid
I.124, 133
III.127
V.91
VI.69
VIII.160
XIII.100
Cure
IV.32
Curiosity
III.209
X.132
Curl
- of Beloved, V.165; XIII.108-9
Current
I.122
spiritual -, IX.16
Custom(s)
III.66
IX.203
XIII.14-7
- at the birth of a child in India, XIII.41-2
- of courtesy, XIII.26
- of drinking the health of friends, XIII.19-20
- of seclusion of women, XIII.20-4
- of the marriage ceremony, XIII.27
funeral -, XIII.39-40
superstitions, - and beliefs, XIII.11-46
wedding -, XIII.39
Cycles
I.30
III.70

Dabistan
XII.129
Dakhl dar makulat
XIII.277
Dance
(see also Raqa)
II.44, 46, 57, 92, 115, 143
III.215
VII.242
VIII.328
-ing soul, I.105
Dandavat
IX.155
Daniel

IV.123, 183, 242
VI.167
VII.50
IX.106, 143
X.113
XIII.265
Dante
VII.18
X.218
XI.166
Dara
VIII.19
Dar-e Sala'm
IX.195, 230
Dargha
II.204
Darguza
(see also Overlooking)
VIII.241-2
Darjeeling
X.193
Darkness
I.27, 111
VIII.321
IX.165
path of -, IX.189
Darwin
VIII.289
XI.67
David
I.33
II.57, 75
XII.133
Day
problem of the -, IX.249
Problem of the - (book), X
Daya
V.193
Dead
influence of the -, V.62
The Living - (play), XII.195-214
Deaf
XI.33
Death
I.80, 117, 119-20, 124, 162, 165-77, 179, 184, 192-6
II.217, 220
IV.22, 41, 46, 107, 161, 192, 211
V.41-7, 107
VI.19, 20, 272-7
VII.185, 194-5
VIII.159-61, 249-50
IX.27, 31-2, 107
X.38, 42
XI.22, 55, 63-4, 237, 240-1, 247-9, 255, 257, 259
artificial means of avoiding -, IV.46
cause of -, V.254
- and hereafter, VIII.170-3
- as inactivity, VIII.175-7, 179-80
die before -, I.195; V.47, 220; VI.27; XIII.104-5
fear of -, VII.229
impression of -, V.42
life after -, V.37-78
living with -, VIII.228
meaning of -, VIII.318-21
other side of -, V.214-6
personal -, VIII.220
Shiva and -, XIII.286-7
warning of impending -, XIII.32
Debts
I.65-6
VI.157, 162
Debussy
II.138
X.229
XII.155
Decay
IX.201
Deception
I.100-1
Deeds
V.41
effect of -, V.210-2
outcome of -, V.210
Defeat
- as success, VIII.72
Degeneration
- of humanity, IX.97, 230
- of religion, IX.241

Deism
IX.69
Deity
- and divinity, IX.116-22
Delhi
X.204
Delicacy
IX.216
Delusion
IV.26
IX.248
Democracy
III.155
VI.47, 55
VII.170-5, 224
IX.30, 121, 126-7
X.91, 244-5, 247
XII.35
religious -, IX.121
spiritual -, VII.176-9
Denial
IV.254
Denseness
IX.39
Dependability
I.90
Dependence
III.122
VII.98, 163, 170, 245-50
VIII.137
IX.105-6
XI.65
XIII.264
- and in-, VII.170
- upon God, IX.105-7
Depression
IX.115, 229
XI.31
Dervish(es)
I.153
II.53-4, 94
IV.63. 121
VI.142
VIII.261
IX.38, 205, 252, 257, 258
XI.159
XII.35, 74, 89, 114, 130
XIII.280
dancing -, XII.113
- in cemetery, XII.141
Desire(s)
I.178, 190, 193, 227-8
II.21
IV.159
VI.19, 73, 195, 203
VII.29, 62, 111, 144, 207-8
VIII.80, 127, 177
IX.83-4, 110, 189
XII.76
XIII.175
bodily -, V.232
changing -, VIII.323
- according to evolution, VII.204
- as longing, VIII.82
- of being, VIII.157, 168
- of God, VIII.127
- of soul, VIII.177-79, IX.26
- shows state of mind, VII.53
five -, I.190-1
four -s of man, III.258
fulfillment of -, VIII.115, IX.84
source of bodily -s, V.232-3
tree of -, I.178
will, wish and -, VIII.80-7
Despair
IX.165
Destiny
VI.146, 172, 216
VIII.136
IX.179
- and free will, VIII.136-44
- of the soul, V.247-56
Destroyer
IX.108
Destruction
I.113
II.213
III.32
VII.14, 118
VIII.285
IX.11, 12, 108, 191, 249
XI.22, 63
contruction and -, V.60
Detachment

I.67, 97
IX.221
Detail
X.190
Deva(s)
I.83, 98-9
II.45
III.132
V.100
VII.80
IX.109, 117
XII.41
Deva-loka
I.136
Devata(s)
I.31
V.100, 125
VII.159
IX.116
Development
- of personality, XIII.169-173
moral -, III.107-8
personal -, X.88
phases of -, III.209-10
spiritual -, II.147-52VIII.28-31
Devil
VIII.97, 104, 129, 145
X.87
Devotee
IX.235
XI.168
Devotion
IV.93
V.19, 28
VII.265
IX.23, 52, 80, 258, 264
XI.167, 188, 190
Dhammapada
XII.137, 140
Dharma
I.145, 213, 217
III.177, 201-2, 221, 227-8
VI.38
VII.199, 206
VIII.157
IX.15-16, 24, 259
XI.173
XII.105, 115
XIII.42
Diamond
XI.23, 67, 109, 138-9
Diet
I.151-2
VIII.298-9
vegetarian -, XIII.213-15
Difficulty, -ies
I.211, 219-21
IV.219
VI.198
IX.35, 184
XI.235
Dignity
III.221
Dilazari
XIII.194
Diogenes
VII.154
Dipak
IV.72
V.91
Direction
X.92
law of -, XI.23
Disagreement
IX.137
Disappointment
I.194, 225
IX.85, 98, 109
XI.153, 233
Disaster(s)
IX.121, 162
Disbelief
IX.83
XI.228
Disciple(s)
I.52
II.239
IV.160, 195
VII.263
IX.245
X.80, 103-10
XI.246, 256
attitude of a -, X.110-14
attributes of -, X.109
- of Jesus, XII.103
- of Muhammad, XII.103

needs of -, X.106-7
Discipleship
IV.203
V.221
IX.245
X.98-105
XI.256
XII.94-105
four kind of -, X.103-9
Path of Initiation and -(book), X.57ff
Discipline
I.52
II.239
VIII.45-8
XII.86
- of consciousness, VIII.47-8
- of mind, IV.160; VIII.47
physical -, VIII.46
self--, 45-8
teaching children -, III.16
Discomfort
XI.244
Discontented
IX.104
Discouragement
XI.153
Discrimination
VI.101
VIII.77-8
Disease(s)
II.47
artificial remedies for -, IV.88
calling -s incurable, IV.42
cause of -, III.97
causes of -, IV.64
chief reason of every -, IV.60-1
nature of -, XI.28
one common cause of all -, IV.75-6
origin of -, IV.69
psychological nature of -, IV.64-71
tracing of -, IV.59-60
Disharmony
I.26
VI.66
results of -, III.124-5
Disheartened
XI.176
Disillusionment
IX.98, 164
Disinterest
-ed attitude, VII.257
Dislikes
XIII.71-2
Disorder
XI.46
mental -, cause of, IV.20
Dispositions
XI.101
Disputes
IX.265
XI.246
religious -, IX.142
Dissatisfaction
XII.16-7
Distress
IX.165-6
Distrust
XI.124-5
Div
IX.117
Divan
X.149, 151
- of Shams-e Tabrez, X.138
Diversity
IX.197
Divine
VIII.258, 264
IX.20, 107, 109, 111, 113, 161, 167, 181-2, 239
- breath, XI.239
- evidence, XIII.55-6
- grace, IX.107
- ideal, IX.266
- impulse, VIII.145
- light, V.251
- love, V.179-87; IX. 229
- manner,IX.111-3, 120
- nature, XI.171
- presence, XI.244; XII.68ff
- spark, IX.118
- Spirit, IX.229
- wisdom, IX.257; XI.150-2

Divinity
I.112, 146
VIII.165
IX.109-10, 116-22, 141-2, 184-5, 206, 242, 249
deity and -, IX.116-22
Divorce
IX.31
Djod
XII.14
Do'a
IV.93
Doctrine(s)
XII.104
Dog
IX.201
-s, VII.89
Dogma(s)
IV.126
IX.22, 161, 264
XII.104
Doing
IX.178
Dome
II.175
III.201
- of God, IX.36
Donkey
VIII.73
Doric
X.205
Dot
I.41
symbology of - and circle, XIII.99-100
Doubt
IV.146, 184
VII.84-5, 88, 91
VIII.258
IX.83, 220
XI.124
XIII.127
- as cause of failure, III.94
Dove
IV.202
IX.223, 225-6
XIII.97
symbol of the -, IX.225-6; XIII.96-7
Dragon
X.180
symbol of -, XIII.106-7
Drama
IX.205
X.232-6
Dreamer
XI.150
Dream(s)
I.39, 142, 173
II.125, 226, 256
IV.149, 200, 210, 226
V.29, 45, 215
VI.148, 216
VII.85, 195
VIII.308-10, 319
-s and inspirations, V.29-30
-s and revelations, IV.210-14
- of life, VII.195
- of the Prophet, IX.230
-ing, VIII.183, 194, 319
five kinds of -s, V.29
real meaning of -s, VIII.319-20
three kinds of -s, IV.226
Drinking
concept of -, X.124
goal of -, IX.201-2
Drugs
IV.33
V.86
VII.108-9
XI.25
XIII.162
Drums
II.46
Duality
I.117, 133
II.85,151, 246
VI.201
XI.44
- of God and man, IX.68
Duija
II.223
Duldul
XIII.28
Dunia
XII.151

Duty, -ies
I.16, 66, 145, 213-17
III.233
VI.34, 37
VIII.157
IX.15, 24, 95, 113, 177, 225, 259
XI.247, 249, 255
XIII.260
- of the faithful in Islam, IX.197
practical -, XI.256
Dvapar Yug
X.223

Eagle
wings of -, (consciousness), IV.229
Earth
I.112, 218
VI.93
IX.217
XI.231
body of -, IX.219
- element, X.161
-ly heritage, I.143-4
sound of -, II.15
East
X.188
XIII.14-5, 17, 24, 26-7
- and West, VI.220; X.41, 258-60; XII.56, 156-9
Eating
goal of -, IX.201-2
Ecclesiasticus
XII.129
Echo
I.168, 235
VI.233
VII.56
IX.36, 66, 149
Economozing
III.200, 223-4
Ecstasy
(see also Wajad)
I.124, 162
II.44, 59, 60, 94, 107, 110, 259
V.32-3
VIII.63-4
IX.110, 220
XI.191
XII.116
- and illumination, VIII.64
five aspects of -, V.32
spiritual -, IX.115
Eden
garden of -, I.223; VII.137
Education
II. 138
VI.109, 110-11
VII.66, 255
VIII.240
XI.216
chief -, XI.136
- at home, III.53
- (book), III.9-114
- of baby, III.34-52
- of child, III.53-74
- of children, III.87-102
- of infant, III.13-33
- of mother, III.21
- of youth, III.14-15, 53, 75-86, 103-113; VI.24
modern -, III.88, 95
moral -, III.98-9
music in -, III.89-90
religious -, III.76
worldly -, IX.150
Ego
(see also Nafs)
I.21, 76, 111, 121
II.26, 246, 251
III.166-7
V.182, 194
VI.87
VII.269, 271
VIII.114, 185, 187-8, 214-5, 228
IX.56, 171, 189, 203, 221, 229, 244
X.19
XI.64, 127, 201-2, 236, 252
XII.83, 85, 90, 95, 97

XIII.171
animal side of man's -, XIII.176-7
constant battle with -, XIII.175-6
- and self-consciousness, XIII.177-8
- and vanity, XIII.178-9
false -, XI.134, 252
jarring effect of - on another, XIII.171-2
man controlled by -, XIII.190
overcoming -, VII.114
psychology of -, XI.202
realization of the true -, XI.201-4
three parts of -, XIII.179-80
three staages through which - develops, XIII.180-2
training of -, XIII.174-192
training of -: and 'Blessed are the poor in spirit', XIII.191-2
training of -: and forgiveness, XIII.190-1
training of -: and humility, XIII.189-90
training of -: necessity and avidity, XIII.182-3
training of -: by abstinence, XIII.183-4
training of -: is as well a science as an art, XIII.185-6
training of -: by refraining from free impulses, XIII.186
training of -: ego is trained as a horse, XIII.186-8
training of -: by not gratifying vanity, XIII.188-9
two sides of human -, XIII.184-5
what - needs and what - does not need, XIII.174-5
what is the -, XIII.172-4

Egotism
I.123

Egypt
IX.170
X.171, 188, 192, 202-3, 215
-ian art, X.181-2, 185
-ians, IX.155
-ian symbolism, XIII.95, 98

Einstein
VIII.200
XIII.280

Elders
I.214-5

Electricity
IV.175
V.91
XI.25

Elementals
II.18, 222
IV.273

Elements
I.112
II.15, 18, 38, 85, 116, 124, 207, 229, 237
IV.28
V.42, 195, 229
VI.118
X.161, 265
colours of -, X.182
- in man, VIII.125
- in the body, V.229
fire -, VIII.201
five -, I.200; IV.28; VIII.167; XIII.215-6

Elephant
II.210
VII.92
VIII.32-3, 70
- fights, IV.244

Elham-e
V.30

Elhami
V.29

Elijah
XII.131

Elocution
II.118

Eloquence
gift of -, VIII.203-5

Emerson
"Beware of what...", I.156

Emotion

II.19, 103
III.79
VIII.280
-al people, XI.176
- of the heart, II.15
-s, V.234
source of -s, V.234

Emptiness
II.262

End
- of the world, V.60-8

Endurance
VII.49
X.46
XIII.256-8
lack of -, VIII.72

Enemy, -ies
VI.66
IX.261
XI.81
dealing with -, III.234-5, 239-40, 243-4

Energy
III.165
IV.35, 167
VI.269

Engineer
IX.175
XI.102

England
XII.154

English
X.94

Enkesar (Enkessar)
VIII.230
XIII.193, 203-4

Enlightenment
IX.32
X.109

Enmity
XI.101, 240
avoiding -, III.252

Enthusiasm
I.94, 179
III.43
VI.205
XI.240

Environment
XIII.282

Equality
IX.199
XI.134
XII.34
- in God's eyes, VII.11-2

Equlibrium
IV.17
XI.244

Error
VIII.216
X.27
- of some religious people, IX.175

Esoteric
VIII.166
IX.249
X.75
- schools, IX.252, 271
- terms, I.38-9

Esotericism
XI.73-4

Essence
II.82
XI.58, 64

Etekad, Rasm u Ravaj
XIII.11-46

Eternal
I.114
VIII.210
XI.158
- and everlasting, XI.153

Eternity
II.73, 148
VIII.16
IX.58-9, 201

Ether
I.112
body of -, IX.219
element, X.161
sound of -, II.16

Ethereal
IX.115

Ethics
I.57-60
III.18

Ettefaq
VIII.234

Eurydice
VIII.191
Eve
Adam and -, II.66; III.161
Everest, Mount
XIII.70
Everyday Life (series)
XIII.207-239
Evidence
IV.53
Evil
I.19, 58-60, 116
VIII.97-99, 104-8, 129
IX.71-2, 163, 255
XI.238, 255
XII.99
definition of -, VIII.104
- thought, IX.229
good and -, IV.109; XIII.174
lord of -, IX.178
resisting -, III.130
"resist not -", VII.48
Evolution
I.135, 230
II.117, 122, 129
IV.125
V.26, 97, 144
VI.236, 240
VII.38-9, 226, 267
VIII.128-30
IX.104, 116-7, 120-1, 161, 166, 179-80, 199, 228, 255
X.172
XI.250
XII.12, 54
- and love, VII.18-9
- of humanity, VII.196
- of soul, VIII.71, 77, 86, 128-30, 161, 164, 172, 289-90
- of world, VIII.168
grades of -, V.25, IX.87
human -, VII.267-71
phases of -, I.237
soul's -, IX.218
spiritual -, I.88-9
stages of human -, IX.65, 68
Exaggeration
XI.138
Exaltation
IV.114
VI.113, 242
VIII.152
IX.28
X.139
XIII.236-7
definition of -, VIII.152
Exercise
physical -, IV.57
Exercises
I.150
IV.160
Exhalation
I.113
IV.131
VI.113-4
IX.102
XIII.163
grades of -, IV.114
Existence
I.111
II.182
planes of -, I.136
Exoteric
IX.249
Expansion
I.113, 143
III.128
IV.124, 235
VI.193
contraction and -, XIII.154-5
Experience
IV.265
VI.118, 257
VII.31
VIII.118
IX.139, 141
XI.146, 229
- of another world, IV.117
-s, pleasant and unpleasant,III.242
influence of -, XIII.67-8
inner -, XI.145
Expert
XIII.278
Expression
II.169, 176, 210, 230

VII.86
VIII.203
IX.36
XIII.59, 76
- and idea, XIII.76-8
Expressiveness
VII.150
Extravagance
XII.58
Eye(s)
IV.83, 91, 215
V.152
VI.55
IX.217
XI.56, 246
XII.27
XIII.60
an - for an -, XI.179
- of the soul, I.16
third -, XI.55-6

Fable
VIII.76
Face
V.95
VII.154
radiance of the -, XIII.233-4
Facts
IV.26, 207
XI.100, 102, 254
Faculties
VI.79
- in disciple, X.107
intuitive -, I.150
Failure
IV.199, 258
VI.201
VII.92
XI.259
- and sucess, IV.104, 199
Fairies
IX.205
Faith
I.48, 60, 226
IV.53, 55, 89
VI.270
VII.32-3, 87-97, 100-1
VIII.41-2, 115, 191
IX.27, 40-1, 52-3, 67, 102, 107, 144, 175, 190, 208, 220, 223
X.105, 114, 146
XI.84, 91, 210-1
XII.42, 100, 123
XIII.245-6
- and reason, VII.95
- defined, XIII.245
- in oneself, XII.100
losing -, VII.87-8
meaning of -, XII.42-6
False
VI.250
IX.107
XI.152, 227
Falsehood
IX.240
Family
IX.262
XI.185-6
- of man, VII.69
Fana
I.39, 42, 184, 205
II.151
V.33, 108, 186, 192
VI.277
VII.187
IX.91, 171, 174, 188
XII.73
--fi-Allah, I.42, V.33, 187; XII.73
--fi-Rasul, I.42, V.33, 186-7; XII.73
--fi-Shaikh, I.42, V.33, 186; XII.73
Faqir
VII.58
IX.252
call of -, XII.113, 130
-s, XI.221; XII.113, 130
Farhad
Shirin and -, V.150-4
Farid-ud-Din Attar
V.22
VIII.14

X.130-3, 137, 216
XI.182, 195
Farishta(s)
II.18
V.100, 113
VIII.119
Farishtakhaslat
I.98
Fasting
VIII.46-7
IX.198
XIII.218
Fate
VI.72
VII.48
- and character, VII.110-18
Father
IX.181, 221
X.122
divine -, IV.277; IX.222
- and Mother of humanity, IX.137
Fault(s)
III.202
IV.100
VI.95, 170, 202, 236, 264
VIII.243, 300
IX.44-5
X.103
XI.198-9
XIII.187, 235
Fear
I.124, 195
II.15, 28
V.43
VI.58
IX.112, 166
XI.124, 165, 234, 257-8
XIII.249-50
purification from -, XIII.237-8
Fearlessness
X.113
XI.117
Feathers
peacock's -, IX.217, XIII.123
Feature
XI.105
Feeling(s)
II.252, 255
IV.125, 142
VI.116, 143
IX.20, 149
XI.35, 74, 90, 109, 230, 232
afraid of -, V.196
consciousness of -, IV.122
consideration of -, XII.87
cultivating -, X.87
Fellow-men
dealings with our -, III.248-50
Female
VIII.94-5
XI.51
- as aspect of God, V.33-6
Few
the chosen -, IX.228
Fikr (Fikar)
IV.87
V.87
X.86
XIII.19, 146-7, 155
Fineness
IV.119
XI.243
Finess
XI.243
Finger
development of power in the - -tips, IV.76-7
healing with the --tips, IV.58-9
shaking the -s, IV.91
Firdausi
V.22, 137
VI.129
X.129-30, 216
Fire
I.112
IX.176, 214, 258
element, X.161
- of the heart, VIII.263
- worship, IX.155
sacred -, VII.23-4
sound of -, II.15
tongues of -, XIII.124-6
Flame
tongues of -, IX.227-8
Flesh

IX.187
XI.122
Flower(s)
IX.118, 216
XI.17, 27, 145
Flute
II.99
IX.216-7, 228, 242
- of Krishna, XIII.122-3
legend of -, VIII.190
Foe
IX.120
Folk-music
X.230
Follower
IX.55
Following
- the message, IX.145
Food
II.212
IV.70
VI.139
XI.64
Foolish
VI.190
VIII.208
- man, XI.108
- people, XI.40
Forces
the two -, XIII.95-6
Ford, Henry
XI.218
Forehead
IX.228
smiling -, VIII.224-6; XIII.266
Forgetting
XI.49
Forgiveness
I.60, 71, 231
III.251
IV.141
VIII.100, 111-2
IX.34, 42-5, 181
XI.233, 244
XIII.190-1, 255-6
- of sins, IX.181-2
Forgiver
IX.94
Form
I.126
II.229
IV.112
IX.101, 120, 148-9, 162, 190-1, 272
X.183
XI.23, 25-6, 56, 105, 191, 242
- of God, IX.113
-s of worship in Islam, IX.196-7
Formlessness
IX.272
XI.191, 242
Fortune
VII.111
Fortune-telling
IV.31
Foundation
- of world's new temple, IX.245
Fountain
sacred -, IX.218
Four
IX.197
Fragrance
XI.30
France
X.205, 254
Francis, St.
VII.147
Freedom
I.82-4, 161, 171, 196
II.79, 100, 145, 239
III.155
VI.155
VII.163-4, 170, 188
VIII.15, 17, 175, 177
IX.65, 221
XI.244, 252, 256
XIII.269
- of action, I.82-4
- of the soul, VII.180-97; VIII.15
kinds of -, VII.193
national -, IX.167
French
X.205

Friday
XIII.43
Friend(s)
I.71
VI.260
VIII.117, 204, 260, 275-6, 263
IX.112
XI.43, 76-7, 100, 189, 207, 247, 251
dealing with -, III.234-5, 239-40, 243-4
- of the messenger, IX.235
- (God), IX.46, 82
how to take dealings of - with us, III.239-40
need of a -, V.185
our dealings with our -, III.234-5, 243-4
Friendliness
manner of -, XIII.193-6, 198
Friendship
I.25, 100
II.83, 86, 211
III.88, 227, 234-5, 239, 243
IV.123
V.185-6
VI.179, 186
VII.151, 251-61
VIII.121, 216, 295, 313
IX.194, 197-8
X.84, 102, 263
XI.207-8, 244, 251
XII.22, 51
- with God, V.186
Frivolity
II.28
III.221
Frossard, Professor
XII.118
Fruit
- as image of soul, VIII.323
Fruitfulness
VI.92
XIII.105-6
Fulfilment
I.191
Funeral
IX.31-2
- customs, XIII.39-40
Future
VIII.217-8
knowledge of past, present, and -, VII.145ff

Gabriel
V.104
IX.149
Gaikwar, H.H. Sayajirao
XII.130
Gain
IX.111
- and loss, VII.119-23
relativity of -, III.258-9
Game
IX.111
Gandharvas
X.222
Ganga
XIII.161
Ganges
II.205
IV.117
VIII.198, 278
X.86, 215
XIII.113
- and Jumna, II.206; IV.117; VIII.278
Garden
- of fragrance, X.216
In an Eastern Rose - (book), VII
rose -, X.216
Gardish-i Dunya
X.198
Garuda
XIII.142
Gathas
IX.146
Gaurakha
XIII.41
Gautama
IX.165-6, 179
Gauth Mohammad
(also Ghauth)

V.22

Gayamat
(see also Peace)
VIII.218

Gayan
IV.287
"All that produces...", VIII.82
"My bare feet...", VIII.142
"If only you explore...", VIII.28
"To repress...", VIII.81

Gayashni
IX.178

Gayatri
IX.150

Gems
VIII.286

Generosity
III.18, 99, 211-12, 216, 257
X.18
cultivating -, III.99
- and greed, III.256-7

Genius
I.124, 129
three stages of -, V.116

Gentleman
VII.29

Gentleness
III.208, 218, 237
VI.48, 78
VII.29, 67
IX.203, 224

George, St.
XIII.106

German
X.226

Germany
X.205

Ghalib
VII.113-4, 154
"I degraded myself...", IX.188

Ghasnavi
VIII.30, 319
X.263
Emperor -, XI.159

Ghauth
(also Gauth)
I.29
V.198
IX.128, 130
XI.216

Ghayrat (chivalry)
III.149-50

Ghazali, al-
V.22, 214
X.61, 111
XIII.31

Ghiza-i-ruh
I.41

Gheirat
XIII.194, 201-2

Ghosts
V.69
IX.205

Gifts
II.212

Girls
abnormality in -, III.

Gita
X.262

Githas
IX.146

Giver
I.175

Giving
I.17
IX.113

Giza-i Ruh
II.59

Glance
I.79
IV.43
IX.213
XIII.54, 109-10
- of the seer, XIII.54-5
healing by -, IV.83

Goal
I.141, 165-85
VIII.151, 194, 327
IX.151, 188, 265
eternal -, IX.172
four paths leading to -, VII.262-6
- of the Sufi, IX.83
journey to the -, V.247-9; VI.253-62; VII.204-11

towards the -, I.165-83
Goats
II.26
God
I.13, 27, 44, 113
V.11-2
VI.123, 213
IX.25-6, 63-122, 139, 149-50, 160, 178, 181-2, 184, 203, 247, 251, 262, 265, 267
X.44-6, 48-51, 86, 88, 93, 95, 105-7, 109, 111, 119, 121-2, 147-54, 159, 168-70, 176, 184, 186, 191, 194-202, 207, 217, 221, 231-2, 243, 248, 254, 258, 265, 269-70
XI.81, 125-6, 139, 147-8, 151-3, 161-2, 162-5, 167, 177-8, 195, 199, 201, 227-8, 230, 232-3, 237-9, 242, 246
abstract -, IX.89-90
action of -, IX.113
altar of -, XI.159
answer of -, IX.36
attainment of -, IX.161
attitude towards -, IX.17
attraction to -, IX.35
attributes of -, XIII.30
awakened within -, IX.85
beauty of -, VII.12, 19-20; XI.193
Being of -, I.115; IX.101, 189; XI.241
belief in -, IV.265; IX.53
believing in -, XII.17
beloved by -, V.12
blaming -, VIII.134
blessing of -, IX.227
breath of -, I.127-8
children of -, IX.140
communication with -, VIII.42, IX.39; XII.73-5
conception of -, VI.185; IX.71-3, 76, 78-9, 80, 85-6, 90, 91; XII.11, 18
condition of -, I.162; XI.247
conscious of -, IX.115
consciousness of -, IV.285; IX.11, 188
creator -, II.185
dealing with -, III.237-8, 242, 252-3
dependence on -, VII.99; VIII.137
dependence upon -, IX.105-7; XIII.264-5
desire of -, I.227
dome of -, IX.37
duty to -, I.215
explaining -, XII.13
external part of -, IX.196
eye of -, I.146
face of-, VIII.118
fatherhood of -, IV.277
feeling of -, IX.20
formless -, IX.195
form of -, IX.113
gate of - (heart), VII.83
gender attributed to -, IX.86
glorifying -, IX.71
- and man, XII.19
- and man, difference between, IX.112
- and Zikar, XIII.19
- a reality, IX.13
- as beloved, XI.248
- as father, XII.72
- as goal, XII.86
- as love, II.146
- as One, IX.101
- as perfection of beauty, II.74
- as person, IX.276
- as personality, V.13
- as spirit, XIII.96
--conscious, IX.51, 66; 157, 163-4, 255
--consciousness, I.14, 30, 145; IX.83
- everywhere, VIII.25
- granting wishes, XIII.36-7
--ideal, VI.184; IX.63-100, 207-8, 215, 258; XI.163
- idealized, IX.116
- idealizing, XII.68-9
- in heart, XIII.29
- in higher intelligence, VII.25

- in man, I.12376
- is all, VII.118
- is eternal, XI.190
- is happiness, XI.244
- is ideal, III.252-3
- is jealous, VII.79
"- is love", IV.55; VII.73; XI.231
- is perfect, XI.250
- is truth, XIII.113
-, Judge and Forgiver, XI.233
- of Islam, the, IX.195-6
- personified, IX.116
--realization, VI.207; IX.195, 209
- realized in life, I.92
-'s dealings with us, III.242; IX.104-5
-, source of intelligence, XI.42
-'s own spirit, IX.184
-'s purpose, I.158, 231, 234
-'s thought, VII.89
- the Absolute, IX.101
- the Father, XIII.170
- the Infinite, IX.101-15
- within, IX.121
greatness of -, IX.96
hand of - in love, VII.14
heart of -, IX.141
idea of -, IX.23-4, 86, 113-5, 204; XII.31
ideal of -, IX.205, 250
immanence of -, I.224; IX.37, 48, 161, 196; XI.231
impulse of -, IX.107
incarnations of -, IX.147
infinite -, IX.101
instrument of -, IX.125-6
Judge and Forgiver, XIII.204
justice of -, VIII.167
kingdom of -, VII.45; IX.96, 192
kingship of -, IX.74
knowledge of -, VIII.181, 256, IX.13, 35, 91, 176, 187, 199, 204, 261, XIII.25
language of -, IX.137
life in -, III.254-5
life of -, I.87; VIII.117-9; IX.230
light of -, IX.120, 140, 242
love of -, I.72-3; III.253; VII.79; IX.171; XI.230
lover of -, I.77
male and female aspect of -, V.33-6
man as aim of -, V.11
manifestation of -, II.54; IX.183; XI.238
manner of -, IX.111, 144; XII.17
man's relation to -, IX.109-11
man, the seed of -, V.131-7; VIII.123-7
message of -, IX.148, 186, 226; XI.233
messemger of -, IX.241
mystic's view of -, X.14-7
name(s) of -, I.121; IX.52, 88, 101, 113, 138, 258
nature of -, VIII.176, IX.103
nearness to -, IX.35
omniscient -, XI.61
one -, XII.71
oneness of -, IX.196
origin of -, XII.14
our dealings with -, III.237-8, 252-3
our - part and our man part, VIII.118-22
our relation to -, XII.68
path to -, XI.161-5
perfection of -, IX.101, 120, XIII.19
personal -, IX.90
personality of -, VII.32-7; IX.67, 70, 86, X.167
personification of -, IX.92
personified -, IX.81
pleasing -, VII.34
pleasure and displeasure of -, III.242
pleasure of -, IV.161; IX.108
power of -, IX.48
praise for -, IX.37, 38
presence of -, I.49, 72;

VII.212-20; VIII.25, IX.39-40, 88, 199, 215, 266
proof of existence of -, XI.171
pupil of -, XIII.13
purpose of -, VIII.127
purpose of belief in -, XI.164
qualities of -, X.93
realization of -, IX.14, 83
recognizing -, XII.69-73
relationship with -, I.70-3; IX.13
sacred names of -, II.35, 66, 157
search for -, IX.85-7
secret of -, IX.13, 151, XIII.259
seed of -, VIII.123-7
self and merit of -, IX.102-4
self of -, IX.51, 101-3
shrine of -, VII.16; IX.193, 229
son of -, IX.120
Son of -, IX.181
spark of -, I.176; VIII.178
Spirit of -, I.116-7; IX.179, 188, 225
state of -, IX.200
Sufi's conception of -, IX.113-5
Sufi's definition of -, III.237; VIII.21
Sufi thought of -, IX.115
sun of -, IX.120
temple of -, I.149
throne of -, IX.234
unity of -, VIII.24
unlimited, II.73
visible -, IX.67
vision of -, IX.256
Vision of - and Man (book), XII.7-124
voice of -, IX.243; XI.254
why on high?, XIII.269
will of -, IV.181; VIII.146, 164; IX.108-9, 134, 192
Word is -, 31, 38
world of -, IX.239
worship of -, IV.287
worshipped as Sun, II.38; VIII.153-4
worshipper of -, XI.163

God-consciousness
IX.115, 131, 144, 160-1, 181
X.91; XI.250

Goddesses
IX.86
XI.177
- of Egyptians, Indians, Greeks, XI.177

Godhead
realization of -, III.170

God-ideal
IX.12, 53, 63-100
XI.253
purpose of -, IX.97
secret of -, IX.81

Godliness
IX.102, 147
heart of the -, IX.119

God-man
XI.164

Gods
IX.86, 88
XI.177
- and goddesses, idea of, IX.204
conception of -, IX.87

God-seeking
- in human heart, IX.20

Gold
V.216
VI.12
IX.214

Golden Age
I.220
VIII.214
X.201, 223
XIII.183

Good
I.58-68
XI.255
- and bad, I.17; V.30, 127; VII.216; VIII.229; XI.242; XIII.226-7
- and evil, IV.108; V.127; XIII.174

Goodness
I.116
VII.55, 215-6
VIII.102, 178, 186, 212, 224, 257
IX.163, 204, 208-9, 255
XI.152, 193, 246
abuse of -, IV.35
path of -, IX.178
Good Shepherd
II.26
Goodwill
VIII.286
Gopis
I.177
II.45
VIII.178
IX.161
Gossip
III.210-11
Gothic
X.205
Governess
influence of -, IV.282
Government
IX.126
spiritual -, I.29
Grace
IV.55
XI.94
Divine -, IX.107, 107
- of God, VII.260
saying -, IX.41
Graciousness
VIII.239-41
Grades
V.25
distinction of -, III.236-7
Grape
IX.218
Gratefulness
III.215-6
Gratitude
V.11
Gravitation
IV.113
VI.227
manifestation, -, assimilation, and perfection, VIII.153-62
Gravity
law of -, VIII.158
Greatness
I.226
X.71
Greece
X.171, 175, 192, 194, 205, 229
XIII.28-32
ancient -, X.187
Greed
I.220
III.256
XIII.174
- and generosity, III.256-7
Greek(s)
IX.155
X.218, 225, 234, 256
XIII.28-32
- mysteries, XIII.29-32
- Orthodox church, XIII.39
oracles among -, XIII.28-9
Gregorian
X.229
Gregory I, Pope
X.229
Grief
II.28
Grihasta
V.121
Gross
- and subtle, IV.113-8
Gruhastha-shrama
VII.209
XII.109
Guidance
I.29
II.166, 254
VI.164
IX.141, 186, 234
X.96
XI.240, 242
divine -, IX.30
parental -, III.186
personal -, IX.271
Spirit of -, IX.127-8, 130, 139-43, 149, 166, 175, 183, 186,

226-8, 240, 242
Guide
I.47
IX.51
choosing a -, I.47-8
- (ing) Spirit, I.14-5
spiritual -, I.94-5
Guimet, Musée
XII.155
Gujerati
- saying, VII.227
Gulfam, Prince
V.161
VII.80
Gulistan
X.142, 144-5
Gulliver's Travels
VIII. 324
Gulman
- and Peri, V.94, 113
Gunas
XI.110
Gunbad
X.204
Guru
II.104, 159, 170, 212, 241
III.15
VI.41
IX.155-6
XII.73, 103
XIII.115
- and chela, XII.94

Habib Allah
IX.147
Habit(s)
VI.135
XI.135-7
- and rhythm, IV.65
Hadi (Guide)
II.66
Hadith
V.56, 180
VII.146
XII.149
Hafiz, Shams-ud-Din
II.79, 87, 159
III.172, 250
IV.94
V.159, 164, 223
VI.35
VIII.14, 17, 122, 161, 228
IX.109, 142
X.77, 123-4, 127, 130, 140-1, 147-54, 216
XI.159, 195
XII.141, 161-2
XIII.35-6, 104, 237, 259
- of Shiraz, X.127
"Before sunrise...", VIII.122
"Sing, my soul...", IX.142
"What comparison...", IX.109
Hahut
I.142
IV.202
V.25
Hairat
X.70
Hajj
IX.198
Hakim
II.64
VIII.255-6
Hal
I.43
II.94, 107
V.86
VI.141
IX.115
Halal
IX.200-2
XII.57
Hali
III.179
Halim
XIII.194
Halima
X.267
Halim Taba'
V.194
Halka
X.86
Hallaj, Mansur al-
IX.110

Hallelujah
II.66
Hallucinations
VII.151
Ham (I or we)
II.65
Hama (praise)
II.65
Hamid (praiseworthy)
II.65
Hamsa
II.64
Hand
III.29
IV.82
V.153
Handwriting
II.81
Hansa
X.213
Hanuman
XIII.17-8
Happiness
I.115, 149, 206
II.83, 232
III.206, 250
V.196, 216
VI.11, 21-2, 28, 114, 121, 158
VII.42, 166, 202-3, 213, 216
VIII.114-7,120, 146-7, 247-8, 256, 272-4
IX.85, 100, 165-6, 225, 249
X.34
XI.145, 150, 197-8, 200, 230, 232-3, 236, 241, 244-5, 248, 258
XII.81
Alchemy of - (book), VI
alchemy of -, VI.11-15
desire for -, I.206-8; VII.156; IX.28
secret of -, VII.42, 45, 55
true - in love, XIII.223
wine of -, VIII.161
Haq (truth)
II.64
V.15, 20
XII.146
Haq al-Iman
I.55
Haqiqat
II.64
VII.35-6
IX.199-200
Haram
IX.200-2
XII.57
Hardship
XI.248
Hariat (bewilderment)
VIII.225
Haris Chandra
(see Stories)
Harmlessness
VIII.142
IX.169, 257
Harmony
I.42, 74-5, 77, 84
II.7, 23-32, 58, 73, 75, 78, 80, 86, 112, 128, 141, 147, 216
III.201, 245
IV.15
VI.50, 66, 73, 125
VII.11, 47, 71
VIII.57-60, 151
IX.13, 15, 20, 22, 48-9, 104, 109, 130, 133, 192, 248, 265
X.53, 186
XI.32-3, 117, 192, 229, 247
XII.39
attainment of -, VIII.59
eternal -, II.23
- and the Sufi, II.31
- and truth, VIII.60
- as beauty, VIII.57
- as rhythm, VIII.58
- between inner and outer action, VIII.152
- between individuals, II.26
- between mates, III.133
- of life, II.28, 30
- of thought, IV.15
- with divine will, VII.47
individual -, II.25
in-, VIII.59

love, -, and beauty, VII.11ff
Sufi keeps -, XIII.224
universal -, II.24

Harp
VIII.275
IX.217

Hassan
XIII.28

Hastani
III.137

Hate
IX.239

Hatha Yoga
IV.151
VII.208-9
XII.103
XIII.187

Hatim
III.223

Haunted places
V.62-6

Hauz-e Kauthar
IX.218

Hauzu 'l-Kausar
XIII.107

Hay (everlasting)
II.65

Haya
XIII.194, 199-200

Hayat (life)
II.65

Hayvanat
VIII.119

Haywanat
V.25

Hayya (modesty)
III.138, 187
al - wa'l iman, III.139

He/she (personal pronouns)
IX.50

Head
VIII.266, 273
IX.36, 202, 228
- and heart, I.150-1
- vs. heart, VIII.269-70
spiritual -, IX.96

Headache
IV.51

Healing
I.171
II.47, 107, 116, 141
IV.41-2, 57, 82, 84-6, 91, 93
VII.17
VIII.71, 269
IX.111
XI.121
absent -, IV.86-7
abstract -, IV.93-4
application of - power, IV.80-7
development of - power, IV.72-9
- at a distance, IV.79
- by breathing, IV.81
- by charms, IV.80
- by glance, IV.83
- by magentic passes, IV.82
- by medicine, IV.82
- by prayer, IV.86
- by presence, IV.85-6
- by suggestion, IV.84-5
- by touch, IV.83
- with finger tips, IV.58
- with music, II.141
- with sound, II.14
- with thought, II.214
mental -, IV.92
origin of -, IV.88-90
physical -, IV.90-2
spiritual -, IV.93
various methods of -, IV.88-94

Health
I.89, 166, 225-6
II.14, 141, 163
IV.11-94, 127, 252
VII.110
VIII.54-6, 298-9
IX.262-3
caring about one's -, IV.48
definition of -, VIII.56
- as self-knowledge, VIII.56
- (book), IV.11-94
- depends on breath, XIII.137
- from spiritual point of view, XIII.219

Hearing
II.128, 177, 185

IX.149-50

Heart

I.26, 42, 44, 47, 59, 79, 91, 123, 136, 143, 235, 238-9
II.56-9, 77, 102, 189, 192, 238, 251, 255
III.219
IV.113, 144, 172, 215, 260
V.11, 145, 230, 243, 256
VI.15, 22, 181, 228
VII.137, 140
VIII.261-5, 271, 279
IX.17, 20, 25, 64, 86, 94, 97, 99, 108-9, 115-20, 128, 131, 137-8, 140-1, 149, 166, 196, 200, 208, 216-7, 222, 227, 229-30, 234, 242, 244-5, 260, 264-5, 267, 276
X.43, 133, 202, 211
XI.81, 197, 230-1, 235, 239, 243-4
XII.57, 86
awakened -, XI.115
conscience as faculty of -, VIII.201
different qualities of -, VIII.269-70
diseases of -, II.252
divine -, IX.141
emotion of -, II.15
expansion of -, IV.259
experience of soul through -, V.243ff
feelings in -, III.251
four aspects of -, V.28
great -, XII.93
- abode of God, VIII.142
- and head I.150-1
- and mind, IV.246; XIII.124, 261
- and soul, V.28
- and wings, IX.20-1, 268-70
- globe over soul, V.256
- of God, IX.141
- of man, VII.16; IX.193; XI.112
- of the godly, IX.119
- of the messenger,IX.240
- of the prophet, IX.145-6, 151
- qualities, IX.258
- quality, IV.113; VI.113, VIII.219, 266-70; XI.112, 115
human -, change in, VII.77
keeping - free from poison, XIII.238-9
keeping - pure, XIII.232-3
kindled -, XIII.57
language of -, IV.141
living -, IV.286; XI.112
magnetism of -, XI.112ff
mind and -, II.251ff
mystical -, X.43-6
poison found in -, IX.193
purification of the -, IX.229, 258
purity of -, XIII.232, 236-7
religion of -, IX.19-20, 25
sensitive -, X.128
tenderness of -, IX.216
tuning of the -, VIII.271-87

Heaven

I.228
II.23, 232
VIII.262
IX.189, 192
XI.234, 240
- and hell, I.179; IV.170, 233, 267; V.53-9; VI.142; VIII.98, 146; IX.192; X.128; XI.231, 234, 240
-s, XI.231
highest -, I.116; XI.240
kingdom of -, V.197; VIII.303

Hebrew

X.215
- mysticism, IX.258
- prophets, IX.176
- religion, IX.164
-s, XI.199

Hegel

V.13

Hell

I.228
II.23, 232
XIII.177

heaven and -, IV.233, 269; V.53-9
- vs. heaven, VIII.98-9

Help
X.97

Helplessness
XI.127, 255

Herbs
XI.25

Hereafter
I.167
IV.258, 269
V.110
VIII.176, 321
IX.189
XI.146, 249
life in -. VIII.75-80

Heredity
V.112, 116
XIII.282
law of -, V.112-20

Heritage
divine -, I.226; XII.26

Hermit
VI.70

Heroes
XI.175

Hidayat (guidance)
II.67

Hidden
IX.95

Hierarchy
IV.259
VII.159, 226
IX.126-7
spiritual -, VII.221-8; IX.96, 125-31, 132-3, 137

Hindi
XI.165

Hindrance
IX.191

Hindu(s)
VI.30
VIII.139, 153, 163, 172, 177, 182, 204, 212, 214, 265
IX.147-8, 150, 161, 206
X.80, 110, 120, 125, 188, 197, 207, 216, 222-3, 233, 246
XI.164, 203
XIII.16-7, 19, 21, 23
- legend, VIII.115
- marriage, XII.40
- masters, XII.133
- poet, VIII.197
- religion, XIII.116
- sages, XII.107-8
- worship, XIII.113
many - gods, XII.32

Hinduism
I.83
IX.155-7, 176
X.253
caste system in -, IX.156-7
forms of worship in -, IX.155-7

Hindustani
X.125, 217-8
- poets, VIII.118-9; XI.162
- song, XII.71

Hira, Gar-e
VII.41
IX.194

Holiness
VIII.211-3

Holy Being
IX.51

Holy Book
I.15-6
IX.196, 267

Home
X.196-7
ideal of -, VII.247

Honesty
III.107
IX.31

Honour
I.23
IX.24, 47-8
XII.53
XIII.201
- of God, XIII.202
-s, I.23

Hope
I.225
IV.40
V.161

VI.195
VII.44, 76
VIII.108, 246
IX.167
XI.83, 252
XIII.246-7
-fulness, I.221; XI.101-2
-lessness, I.226, IV.40; XI.83, 88

Horizon
VIII.114, 243
IX.54
XI.228, 252, 257

Horoscope
XIII.46

Horse
XIII.27-8, 148
- like ego, XIII.186

Hosh ba dam
XIII.152

Hosh bar dum
XII.141

Hospitals
IV.37

Hotel
- life, XI.185

Hu
II.64

Huda
II.67

Hudd (limitation)
II.67

Huma (tree)
II.65
IX.175

Huma manam
I.57
V.192

Human (being)
I.140
II.27
VII.52-3, 72, 75
VIII.235-7, 239
IX.51
X.95
XI.245
XII.36
angelic -, II.27
animalistic -, II.27
devilish -, II.27
form of -, IX.205
four varieties of -s, III.131
- mind, II.47, 120, 145
- vs. divine, VIII.165
kingdom of -, II.13, 186
nature of -, III.207; IX.21, 28, 112, 116, 165, 187, 205, 223, 253; XI.156, 170, 179, 184, 198, 204, 245
original meaning of -, II.65
personality of -, IX.86, 118, 249
privlege of being -, VIII.113-7
virtue of -, greatest, IX.119

Humanity
I.89-90
IX.11, 118-9, 185, 263
XII.59
cry of -, IX.130, 269
degeneration of -, IX.97, 230
lessons of -, IX.207
present condition of -, IX.255
progress of -, IX.230
state of -, IX.12

Humiliation
IV.143
VIII.202, 228
IX.90
XI.160
XIII.233

Humility
I.75, 205
IX.34, 96, 197, 203, 224
XI.99-100, 159, 227
XIII.189-90
blessing of -, XI.160
- in Bible, Qur'an, ancient Rome, XII.69

Humming
IV.20

Humour
VI.58
X.144
XI.247

Hunger
IX.93

Hu
XIII.181
Hur (heavenly beauty)
II.65
V.113
Huris and Malaks
V.54
Hurt
IX.108
Hussein
XIII.28
Huvva (Eve)
II.65
Huwal (omnipresence)
II.65
Hyderabad
VIII.196, 209
X.106
sage in -, XII.63
Hypocrisy
XI.148
Hypnotism
IV.42

I
XI.151, 203
Iblis
I.123
Ida
XIII.95
Idea
-s, II.150
expression and -, XIII.76-8
symbology of religious -s, IX.213ff
word and -, XIII.75-6
Ideal
I.16, 18, 31, 42-4, 72, 88, 173, 176
II.21, 58-60
VI.107, 246-52, 246-52
VII.23, 219
VIII. 23
IX.17-18, 20, 26, 51, 58, 82, 97-100, 109, 110, 121-2, 159-60, 172, 181, 188, 245, 249, 255, 264, 267, 272, 277
XI.158-9, 160, 173-8, 255-6, 258
XII.45
application of -, IX.99
breaking the -, III.126
divine -, IX.92, 174, 266
God as -, VIII.26
God -, IX.63ff
- behind idol, VIII.79
- beyond explanation, VII.101
- life, VII.198-203
- of art, X.175-9
- of friendship, VIII.295
- of God, IX.205, 250
- of mystic, XI.166-8
- of prophet, IX.145
- of soul, VIII.178
- of Sufi, I.13; IX.264-6; XII. 29-32
-s, XI.236
-s, on some, III.126-30
mystical -, XI.187
national -s, III.128-9
religious -, IX.22-3
seeking for -, IX.26-9
spiritual -, IX.129; XI.140
Sufi -, XII.29-32
true -, X.111
Unity of Religious -s (book), IX
Idealism
VII.170-1
IX.90, 97-100, 164, 204
X.99
Idealist
I.143
Identity
purification from -, XIII.239
Idol
I.44
VII.41, 218
VIII.79
IX.77, 204, 208, 239
XI.255
-s, VII.218
- worship, VII.41; IX.82

Idolatry
IX.77-8, 167, 204-10
Ignorance
I.19, 34-5, 39, 146, 165
V.19
VI.80, 120
VIII.142
IX.88, 104, 106, 190, 203, 221, 234, 241
XI.18, 116, 180, 247-9
- cause of fear, XIII.251
wisdom and -. V.217-18
Illness
II.143, 164
IV.15, 24
VII.185
IX.165, 181-2
X.251
XI.29, 46
XIII.227-8
denying -, IV.27
impression of -, XIII.227
mental -, IV.21
physical -, IV.21
root of -, IV.26
undesirable -, XIII.229-31
ways of looking at -, IV.45
Illumination
VIII.28
IX.120, 173-4, 185, 226-8, 258
XI.248
Way of - (book), I.9ff
Illusion
I.184
VI.124, 127
VIII.317
IX.18, 85, 107, 224
XI.15-9, 152, 227, 249, 257
- and reality, XI.15-19
nature of -, XI.16
Ilm
V.87, 88, 143
Ilmi Adab
XIII.193
Ilmi Rabbali
XIII.30
Image
IX.167-8
- of God, I.126; VIII.116; IX.37, 139
Imagery
Sufi poetic -, X.123-5
Imagination
I.39, 70, 157, 167
II.15, 226, 251, 255
III.77
IV.48, 135, 148, 157, 210
VII.84
IX.52, 66-7, 91-2, 98, 106, 115, 117, 176, 206
XI.56, 138, 146-7, 227, 250
XII.24, 60
XIII.262
- and intuition, VII.84
- and thinking, IV.158
thought and -, II.226ff
Iman
I.55, 203-4
IV.89
VI.211
VII.90
VIII.270
XIII.55
Iman-e Kamil
I.55
Iman-e Muhmil
I.55
Imitation
II.114
IX.151
X.102
Immanence
Divine -, VIII.242; IX.37, 43, 161, 176, 196, 207, 258; XIII.32
Immaturity
I.51-2
Immensity
X.42
XI.164
Immortality
I.21, 167, 195
II.151
VI.273
VII.147
VIII.49, 181

IX.28, 217-8, 221, 267
XI.65, 245
Imperfection
IX.91
XI.220
-s, V.196
Impoliteness
XI.137
Importance
IX.126
Impression(s)
I.39, 129-30, 171, 174, 181
II.106, 115, 209ff, 228, 254
III.69, 158-9
IV.27, 65, 102, 107, 222, 248, 252
V.92, 114, 136
VI.147, 170
VII.83
IX.52, 119, 141, 149, 229
XI.80-4, 86, 94, 105, 124-5, 258
XII.38
XIII.63-4, 221-2, 228
first -, XI.107
perceiving -, VI.127
rejecting -, XIII.235
suggestion through - and belief, XI.80ff
undesirable -, IV.101; XIII.229-31, 234
Impulse
II.242, 256
III.218-9
VI.64, 66, 102, 204
VII.55
VIII.52, 81, 145-9
X.20
definition of -, VIII.148
divine -, IV.161; VIII.145-9, IX.107, X.20
- from God, VII.89
-s, XIII.186
process of -, VIII.147-8
spiritual -, IX.82
In an Eastern Rose Garden
(book), VII
XII.76
Inayat Khan, Hazrat
confessions of -, XII.125-163
early life, XII.129-31
Eastern training, XII.160-3
- and East and West, XII.156-9
- and Islam in youth, XII.130
India tour, XII.136-9
initiation in Sufism, XII.146-50
interest in Sufism, XII.140-5
study of religions, XII.132-5
tour in the West, XII.151-55
Incarnations
- of God, IX.147
Incense
IX.176, 258
Inclinations
VI.25
VII.162
Independence
III.29
VIII.247, 275
IX.105
XI.65, 199
XIII.264
- and dependence, VII.170
India
VII.102
IX.148, 150, 156, 161, 164
X.84, 99, 131, 180, 182, 187-8, 192-3, 202, 216, 224, 226-8, 253, 252
XII.152
XIII.11-2, 17, 21-2, 28, 30, 33
Indian(s)
X.227
XIII.11-2
Indifference
I.99-100
II.28
III.200
V.27
VI.40, 174
VIII.247, 259, 264-5, 291, 325
IX.95
X.94-5
XII.92
interest and -, V.27

power of -, VI.176
Individuality
I.130, 136-7
II.100
IV.107, 271
VI.44, 78
VII.53
VIII.162, 167, 232
XII.16, 33
Indra
VII.243
X.151
court of -, III.215, 226; VII.243
Indra Loka
I.127
VII.80
X.222
Indra Sabha
V.161
Inertia
IX.100
Infancy
III.28
VII.193
XI.154-5
Infant
IX.104
XI.116
XII.15
angelic qualities in -, III.28
caretakers for -, III.31
controlling -, III.15
crying of -, I.182; III.17,25,30
education of -, III.13-33
education of - before birth, III.26
ethics for -, III.18
excitement of -, III.17
habits of -, III.31-3
relaxation of -, III.19
rhythm of -, III.21, 23
silence for -, III.23-4
soul of -, III.13
sounds of -, III.24
standing and walking of -, III.20-21
teeth of -, III.20
temperaments of -s, III.33
training of -, III.23
Infinite
XI.247
tuning with the -, IX.194
Influence
I.26
IV.277, 282-3
V.62
VI.62
VII.150
VIII.227
- of other minds, VII.53
soul radiates -, XIII.82-3
Inhalation
I.113
XIII.163
Inharmony
IX.169
Inheritance
IV.275-7
IX.120
divine -, IX.66
- from God, XII.65
Initiation
I.46-53, 202
II.117, 181, 202, 249
IV.203
VIII.307
IX.128, 131, 137, 230
X.51, 61-86, 88, 91, 93, 97
XI.121, 248
XII.21, 50, 64
advanced -, X.92
conditions of -, I.50
higher -s, IX.193; X.92
- in God, X.68-9
meaning of -, X.71-7
natural -, X.92
path of -, X.61-70
Path of - and Discipleship (book), X.57-114
prerequisites for -, I.48
three aspects of -, X.91-7
Initiative
X.92
Initiator
X.90

Injustice
XI.162
Innocence
I.68-9, 89, 116-7
III.184
IX.66, 111, 141
XI.116, 134, 141, 180, 240
XII.15
XIII.234-5
- of infant, X.94
- real purity, XIII.234
Inoculation
IV.16
vaccination and -, VIII.249-50
Insan
V.25
Insanity
IV.24, 67-8
Insects
II.27
Insight
I.236
II.81
IV.44, 184, 215-28
VIII.43-4
IX.214
XIII.51-86
three ways to develop -, XIII.83-5
Insincerity
IX.120
Inspiration
I.39, 185, 122, 131
II.74, 81, 118, 193, 206, 242, 259-62, 295
IV.224
V.29, 245
VI.128, 148
VII.85
VIII.259
IX.16, 92, 139
X.109, 112, 120-1, 126-7, 187
XI.220, 230
XIII.148, 158
divine -, IX.140
five kinds of -, V.29
- and power of mystic, XI.220-3
-s, dreams and, V.29-30
Instrument(s)
XI.251
- of God, VIII.116, 148; IX.125-6
- as machine, VIII.165
percussion -, II.15, 57, 110
stringed -, II.57, 101, 103, 110
wind -, II.15, 57, 99, 110
Intellect
I.38, 200
II.165
V.20, 28
VII.233, 262
VIII.279
IX.66, 103, 166
- and wisdom, V.28; VII.233-8
Intellectual
I.93
Intellectuality
IV.142
XI.110
Intelligence
I.23, 28-9, 38-9, 54, 113, 125, 160, 162-4, 178, 181, 232
II.37, 43, 233, 249
III.119
IV.39, 123, 229
V.143
VII.25, 189, 262-3
VIII.40, 131, 289, 296, 316
IX.57, 94, 103, 141, 166, 192
XI.38, 40, 41-3, 60, 64, 66, 231, 241, 243
XII.81
clear -, VIII.298; XI.218
dense form of -, XI.41
divine -, VIII.30; IX.182
higher -, IX.183
human -, XI.42
- and consciousness, VIII.289, 316-7
- is light, XII.80
- of God, XI.38
- of planet, XI.41-2
light of -, VIII.153
omnipresent -, IX.179
pure -, VIII.289; XI.38, 59, 69

source of -, XI.42
supreme -, III.119-20
Intensity
II.213
Intention
IV.57
V.89
IX.108, 178
Interest
V.27
VI.174, 176
XIII.80
- and indifference, V.27; VI.174-81
- in all things, XIII.80-1
Interference
IX.271
Interpretation
X.130
Intolerance
VII.268
XI.254
XIII.173, 293
Intoxication
I.65, 184
II.63, 76
III.227-8
VI.133, 139, 141
VIII.122, 179
IX.94, 97, 110, 112
X.201
XII.48
four kinds of -, I.180
- of activity, VIII.209
- of life, VI.133-44
Intoxicants
IX.201
XIII.217
Intuition
I.39, 125, 150, 190
II.81, 89, 96, 125, 139, 141, 169, 173, 192, 213, 218, 230, 253, 255
IV.32, 44, 222
VI.126-7, 148
VII.82-6, 235-6
IX.149, 214, 218
X.48, 171-2, 188-9
XI.90, 196, 229
XIII.55, 68-9, 107, 253
centres of -, XI.21
Invocation
IX.50
Involution
VI.240
VIII.214
Iqbal
"I wandered...", I.22; VIII.332
Iraqi
VIII.188-9
V.182
Ireland
XIII.32
Iron Age
VIII.214
X.223-4
XIII.183
Irregularity
- of breath, XIII.147
Irritation
VIII.69
XIII.185
Isaac
IX.170-1
Ishmael
IX.170, 193, 198
Ishq
V.88, 143
Ishq Allah Ma'bud Allah
V.17, 144
XI.188
XII.141
Ishwara
VII.12
Islam
I.56
V.209
IX.155, 164, 195, 247, 264
X.123, 253
XII.130, 133
XIII.28, 30
duties of faithful in -, IX.197-9
essential teaching of -, IX.196
forms of -ic worship, IX.196f
four grades of knowledge in -,

IX.199
God of -, IX.195-6
idea of Halal and Haram in -, IX.200-02
worship in -, IX.196-7
Ism-e Asam
XII.118, 122
Ism-e Azam (name of Most High)
II.64
Israel (Jacob)
I.121
II.36
Israelite
IX.258
Israfil
V.104
Israil
V.104
Italian
X.205
Italy
IV.164
X.175, 218, 227

Jabrut
I.141-2
IV.201
V.25
Jacob
I.121
II.36
IX.221
- wrestling with angel, I.121; IX.221-2
Jafar
II.358
Jagarji Chandra Bose
(see Bose)
Jagrat
IV.198
Jain
- hymn, XII.158
Jainism
IX.169, 257
Jalatarang
II.15
Jam
I.49
Jam-e Jamsheyd
IX.218
Jam-e Kauthir
I.180
Jami
V.180
VII.254
VIII.14, 17, 228, 271
X.130, 133
XI.159, 195
XII.133
Jamsheyd
I.49
IX.218
-, king of Persia, XII.71
Jannat
I.167-8
V.54
VIII.175
Japan
X.181, 201, 203
Jayadev
III.172
Jazz
II.44, 93, 105, 110
Jealousy
III.149
IX.127
XI.237
Jebrael, Jebrail
(see also Gabriel)
V.104
IX.230
Jehovah
II.66
Jelal
I.121
II.22, 34, 59, 115
IV.284
V.231
VII.74, 143
IX.127, 127
X.205
XI.132
XIII.95, 160

- and jemal, VII.236-7
- as creative power, VIII.94

Jelal-ud-Din Rumi
II.15, 46, 59, 85, 95, 187, 207, 237
III.254
IV.114, 132, 263, 278
V.13-4, 22, 32, 122, 145, 164, 242
VI.259
VII.38-9, 59, 75-6, 130, 137, 139, 146, 180, 207, 243
VIII. 14-5, 132, 190, 192
IX.48, 75, 151, 216-7, 242
X.127, 130-1, 134, 137-41, 216
XI.62, 195
XII.16, 74, 114, 135, 151, 157
XIII.122-3, 150
"Even the spider...", IX.93
"Every night...", I.196
"Hail to thee...", I.19
"Man...causes...", IX.48
"People are drawn...", I.117
"Something which...", I.161
"The Beloved...", IX.114
"Through fire...", IX.48
"Whether you ...", VIII. 259, 287; XI.189-90

Jelani, Abdul Qadir
(also Jilani)
V.206

Jemal
I.121
II.22, 34, 115
V.231
VII.74, 143
IX.125, 127
X.205
XI.132
XIII.95, 160
- and jelal, VII.236-7
- as responsive power, VIII.94

Jerusalem
IX.195

Jesus Christ
I.21, 33, 46, 90, 143, 167, 205
II.26, 160, 244
VI.36, 38, 39, 79, 88, 122, 186, 236, 245
V.194
VII.14-5, 32, 68, 71
VIII.19, 37, 68, 329
IX.16, 23, 24, 30, 94, 109, 118-9, 121, 125, 141, 147, 150, 170, 172, 181-2, 179-92, 208, 215, 226-7, 233-4, 236, 238, 240, 242, 244, 247, 255, 257, 261, 264, 266, 270, 271-2, 277
X.16, 18, 27, 29, 44-5, 62, 67-8, 72, 75, 95-6, 98, 101, 109, 136, 140, 146, 154, 241, 253-4, 262-3, 267
XI.122, 141, 166, 185, 227, 245, 252, 254
XII.133
XIII.18, 25, 32
Beatitudes of -, IX.189-90, 244
"Before the cock crow...", IX.223
"Be ye perfect", I.91, 228; VI.182, 218; VII.43, 56; VIII.18, 162; IX.74, 91, 113, 142, 182; XIII.32; XII.50
"Blessed are the meek...", I.123; VIII.239; XI.232
"Blessed are the poor in spirit", V.194-6; VIII.103, 188; XIII.171, 186, 191-2
"Blessed are they that mourn...", V.196-7
blood of -, XIII.25
"...born again...", VI.259
"Call me not good", IX.241; XIII.255
"Consider the lilies...", IX.93
cross of -, VIII.184-90 ; XIII.94-5
crucifixion of -, I.84, VIII.38; IX.182
"Do unto others...," I.18
"Eat my flesh", XIII.25, 129
essemce of teachings of -, VII.40
flesh of -, XIII.25
"Fishers of men", XIII.129,

203
"Follow me...", IX.118
"Forgive us ...", IX.45
forgiveness of -, VIII.100
habitation of -, IX.64
"He who taketh the sword...", XIII.259
"I am Alpha...", I.34; IX.183, 186, 238, 247
"I am the Way...", VIII. 326
"I and my Father...", VII.25
ideal of -, IX.182
immaculate birth of -, IX.181
- called God 'Father', XIII.52
- ideal man, VII.115-6
- in wilderness, VII.41
- on eternal life, VIII. 249
- on faith, VII.59, 92
- on fatherhood of God, IV.277
- on spiritual democrary, VII.175
- riding on donkey, VIII.73
- to fishermen, VII.75
- walking on water, VII.184; VIII.107-8, 248; IX.222-3, XIII.120
"Judge not...", I.157; III.225; VIII.147, 242
"Let those throw a stone...", XIII.255
life of -, VIII.126, 143
light of -, IX.183
"Light under a bushel...", IX.12, 117
love of -, IX.222, 228
"Love your enemies", VIII.133, 214
manner of -, VIII.264
"My Father's house...", XII.92
mystic's view of -, X.15
personality of -, VIII.235; XIII.124-5
"Poor in spirit", (see "Blessed are the ...")
religion of -, IX.164
"Render unto Caesar...", III.262
"Resist not evil", VI.102; VIII. 57; XIII.190, 254
resurrection of -, VIII.181-3
second coming of -, I.45-6
"Seek ye first...", I.204, 235; VI.261; VII.153; VIII.116, 274; XI.150
Sermon on the Mount, XIII.225
soul of -, IX.139, 240
spirit of -, IX.179, 228
teaching of -, VI.20; XII.59
teaching of - and dervishes, XII.114
"The spirit quickeneth...", IX.187; XIII.41, 212
"Think not...", IX.21, 30
thought of -, XII.89
"Thy kingdom come...", IX.96
"Thy will be done...", I.227; VI.216; VIII.143, 145-6, 221 172; X.191-2
"Turn other cheek...", XIII.102
"Where your treasure is...:, IV.270; IX.268
word of -, IX.64
words of -, VIII.38, 235

Jewels
II.207
IX.214

Jew
XI.164

Jewish
X.257
- mysticism, VIII.19
- scriptures, IX.146

Jibra'il (Gabriel)
XIII.121

Jilani, Khwaja Abdul Qadir
(also Jelani)
II.203
V.22
"I am the bird...", IX.187

Jili, al-
"If you believe...", IX.104

Jinn
(see also Planes)
I.98-9, 124-32, 169, 171, 174-9, 233

V.108, 110, 114
VI.226
VII.16
XI.154, 252
communication with -, I.131-2
- qualities, I.90-1, 136-7; XI.157
-s, V.113; IX.205; XII.14
- sphere, I.138-9; VII.241

Jivan Mukhta
V.121

Jnana
I.125
VI.27
VII.210

John, St.
"Without Him was not anything made...", IX.48

John the Baptist
II.26
X.62, 72

Joseph
I.33
X.122
XII.133

Journey
I.65, 184
V.98, 247
VI.161, 259
VII.204
IX.83, 216
XI. 133, 233
inner activity, VIII.150
- and symbol of cross, VIII.184-5
- of the soul, VIII.176
- to the goal, V.247-89; VI.253-62; VII.204-11; VIII.180
- towards spiritual ideal, VIII.184
life's -, X.111; XI.153-7
object of the -, I.70-3
preparation for -, I.65-9
spiritual -, I.67

Joy
I.185, 232-3
II.17, 231, 259
III.163
VI.122
VII.29
VIII. 180, 186, 306, 328
IX.214, 229, 246
X.100, 112
XI.197-8, 229, 250, 252
body of -, IX.219
- in union, VIII.15
plane of -, IX.220

Judaism
IX.170, 200-1
X.253

Judge
IX.94

Judging
I.82, 157
V.48
VIII.109-12
XI.239
X.52

Judgment
I.59-60, 82-3
II.243
VII.62
VIII.109-12
IX.17, 43, 72, 145, 266

Judgment Day
I.168-9
IV.252
V.48-52
IX.17, 94
XI.230, 232
XIII.279

Juggler
XI.222

Jumma Shah
XII.129

Jumna
II.205
XIII.161

Juneyd-e Baghdadi
V.22

Just
becoming -, XI.205

Justice
I.17, 65, 71, 168
III.224-5, 238

V.48
VII.164
VIII.106, 110, 285
IX.45, 94, 267
XI.76, 180, 230, 231, 233, 238
XIII.250-251
divine -, IX.32
- of God, VIII.110-1

Ka'ba
II.202
IV.53
VI.192
Kabala
X.262
Kabir
I.148
V.85, 221
VI.117
VIII.20, 295, 329
XII.152
XIII.203
Kabs
XIII.154
Kadr and Kaza
IV.16, 161, 179, 181
V.60, 218-9
VI.223
VII.46, 120
VIII.49, 69,82
XIII.273-5
Kafir
XII.134
Kaiser
X.190
Kala (time)
II.40, 55
Kalam
V.28
Kalamat
IX.196
Kalam-ullah
IX.147
X.69, 140
Kalanki
XIII.28
Kali
IX.87, 235
X.65
Kalidasa
VIII. 329
X.233
Kali Yug
X.223
Kalpa Vraksha
VII.135
Kama
VII.206
IX.259
Kamana Kalpa Vriksha
XIII.111
Kaml
IX.207
Kamsa
IX.162
X.267
Kam Sukham
XIII.194
Karima
X.141-2
Karma
I.137, 176
II.35
V.124-6
VI.123
VII.243
VIII.110, 134, 139, 140-1, 143, 163-72
IX.168
XIII.288
- and reincarnation, VIII.163
Karobi
XIII.95
Kashf
XIII.51-86
Kasif
XIII.142
Kavi Ratnakar
XII.130
Kaza and Kadr
IV.16, 161, 179, 181
V.50, 60, 218-9
VI.223
VII.46, 120, 129

VIII.49, 69, 82
XIII.273
Kemal
I.30
II.22, 34, 115
III.75
V.60
VII.143, 237
IX.134
X.205
XI.132-3
XIII.45, 95, 101, 162
Kemal Pasha
IV.164
Key
- to prophetic path, IX.151
Khaak
I.112
V.26
Khair
I.120
Khairulmubin, Maulana
XII.147
Khalif
I.29
-s, V.222
-s of Muhammad, IV.284
Kham (shame)
XIII.289-90
Khamush
IV.217
Khan, Inayat
(see Inayat Khan)
Khan, Maheboob
(see Maheboob Khan)
Khan, Mir Mahebub Ali
(see Nizam of Hyderabad)
Khan, Mohammed Ali
(see Ali Khan)
Khan, Musheraff
(see Musheraff Khan)
Khanda
II.45
Khar
I.120
Khatija
III.178
IX.194
Khatija Bibi
XII.129
Khatim al Mursalin
V.20
Khatir
XIII.193, 198-9
Khaunda Pishani
XIII.266
Khayali
V.29
Khayyam, Omar
II. 232
V.22, 58
VI.38, 58, 257
VII.56, 89, 132
VIII.14, 16-7
XII.59
XIII.104
"A hair perhaps...", I.120
- on heaven, XII.76
"Oh my beloved...", I.229
Khidr
II.242
Khilvat dar najuman
XII.141
Khuda
IV.214
X.50
Khulk
VIII. 239-40
XIII.193
Khusru
VII.172
XI.163
Khwaja of Ajmer
II.203
Kibria
III.220
VI.57
XIII.201, 203, 293
Kimia, al-
V.216
Kindness
III.28, 248, 251
VII.55
IX.257
XI.202
King

VIII.227
IX.94-7, 111
- of kings, IX.97
-ship of dervish, XII.142-3
Kingdom
VIII.203
animal -, VII.74; XI.156
- of God, I.176, 204, 235; II.223, 249, IX.96, 19; IV.6, 35; V.197, 223; VII.75; VIII.116, 259; XI.233
- of man, VIII.135
-s, VIII.124; IX.112
-s of creation, VIII. 128-9
mineral -, II.13, 186; VII.73
Rumi's version of -, VIII.131
vegetable -, I.28, 90, 111, 135; II.13, 186; VII.73
Kingliness
IX.95-6, 111
Kismet
VII.134
Kneeling
IX.202
Knights of Purity
V.21
Knower
I.232, 234
IX.125
XI.50
Knowing
I.199, 240
XI.50
Knowledge
I.39, 68, 95, 125, 145, 198-9, 224, 232
II.33, 151, 162, 233
III.75
IV.121, 123, 142, 249
V.249-50
VI.21, 53, 78, 114, 201, 260
VII.146, 162
IX.54, 103, 125, 139, 199, 233, 261
X.24-5, 73, 107-8, 133, 175
XI 50, 146, 196, 243, 249
centre of -, IX.228
desire for -, I.198, 202
essence of -, XI.145
kinds of -, VIII.272-3
intellectual -, VIII.284
- of God, I.20; VI.15; IX.35, 167, 192, 261; XI.249
- of past, present, future, VII.145-8
- of spiritual stages, I.95-6
- of the self, IX.110
- of where one is going, VIII.151
soul's -, VIII.300-1
spiritual -, XI.243
sublime -, VII.229-32
sweetest aspect of -, XI.145
Konya, Turkey
(see Qoniya)
Kosh
X.212
Kotah Kalam
XIII.194
Krishna
I.177, 230
II.15, 45, 54, 75
III.177
V.198
VII.26, 71, 265
VIII.37
IX.30, 143-4, 146, 160-3, 173, 179-80, 186, 216-7, 233, 241, 264, 269
X.16, 67, 188, 227, 253, 267
XI.167, 194, 227
XII.161
XIII.28
flute of -, II.62; IX.216-7; XIII.122-2
- and the Gopis, VIII.178
- Girdhara, VIII.182
"We appear...", I.34
Krita Yug
X.223
Kshatrias
IX.156
Kshattria
V.125
Kudsi
IV.267

Kufi
VIII.20, 22
Kumkum
IX.215
XIII.113
Kunashni
IX.178
Kun ba Ismi
IV.90
Kun ba Ismi Allah
IV.90
Kundalini
XIII.140
Kursi
V.28
Kurus
IX.162
Kusha
VII.63
Kushtam (wrestler)
VIII.92
XII.71

Labor
XII.54
La elaha ill'Allah
I.33
Lahu
VII.63
XIII.28
- and Kusha, VII.129
Lahut
I.142
V.25
Lakshmi
I.207
IX.207
X.185
Lamb of God
II.26
Lamps
IX.226, 272
Language
I.85, 119, 183
II.34-5, 50-1, 89, 92, 96, 121, 131, 169, 179, 189
IV.113, 141
VII.147
IX.135, 228
XI.90, 114
XII.121
ancient -s, IV.113; XI.90
cosmic -, II.189-95
Cosmic - (book), II.189-262
divine -, I.85-6
human -, XI.171
- of God, IX.137
- of the mind, XIII.66
-s, XII.121
Lassia Nrutya
II.45
Latif
XIII.142
Latin
X.218
Lauwama
V.25
XI.202
XII.34
XIII.181
Law
I.85, 137, 177
V.30, 60, 198
VI.233-8
VII.55
VIII.132, 150
IX.30-3, 94, 102, 173-4, 186, 237
X.17-8
XI.179, 231, 258
divine -, I.16, 17; IX.30, 137, 173, 200
five aspects of -, IX.31
- of action, V.30-1; VI.233-9
- of attraction, VIII.91
- of beneficence, VIII.243-53
- of God, XI.256
- of heredity, V.112-20
- of inner life, I.85-92
- of karma, VIII.165
- of life, VIII.150-2; IX.174
- of reciprocity, III.233-42
- of religion, IX.30-33
- of renunciation, III.254-62

- of rhythm, XI.44-8
- vs. love, VIII.111
-s, XI.179
-s, common and inner, I.84
-s of ethics, III.126
-s, worldly, I.83
making -, IX.32-3
natural -, VIII.145

Lawh
V.28

Layam
IX.174

Laziness
VIII.83
XI.128

Lazy
XI.137

Lazzat
V.26

Leader(s)
I.28-9
VII.222-3

Leaf
VIII.293

League of Nations
VII.177

Learning
I.66, 93, 156, 198-200
II.151
VI.190
VII.234, 263
IX.15
X.21, 108
XII.26
artificial -, I.224
inner -, VI.21
- and unlearning, VII.244; X.21

Leaves
IX.239

Legend
IX.218
XI.150

Leila and Majnun
III.140
V.171-8
VI.185
VII.219, 261
IX.23
X.175
XIII.117-20

Lessons
XII.104

Liberation
I.115
V.46
IX.181
XI.258
spiritual -, IX.167

Liberty
IX.205
Statue of -, IX.167
Sufi Message of Spiritual - (book), V.9ff

Lies
XII.31

Life
I.21, 24, 39, 67, 138, 166, 177, 228
II.87, 121, 140, 142, 148, 151, 190, 214, 220, 251
III.95, 198, 211, 261
IV.75, 82, 152, 162
V.50, 212
VI.16, 24, 27, 40, 72, 76, 82, 87, 151, 154, 159-60, 192, 272
VII.38, 40, 113, 136, 150, 162, 218
VIII.331
IX.14-15, 52, 97, 100, 104, 107, 112, 159-61, 165, 172, 180-1, 222, 248, 262
X.49, 89, 128, 146, 202, 243
XI.22, 26-7, 63, 65, 115, 123, 150, 160, 176, 212-3, 234, 241, 243, 247, 249, 250, 252-3, 255, 257
XII.104
XIII.284-6
aim of -, VI.16-23
Aqibat, - after Death (book), V.37-78
attainment of the inner -, I.93-7
balance of -, XIII.64-6

communicating with -, VI.126-32
condition of -, IX.12
confidence in -, VIII.280
continuity of -, VI.272-7
culmination of -, XI.158
deeper side of -, VI.103-8, VIII.219-20
desire for -, VII.157-8; IX.26-7
divine -, IX.15, 111
eternal -, I.39, 87; VII.184; IX.201, 216
everlasting -, I.19
evolution in -, IX.199
four motives in -, IX.259-60
fulfilment of the obligations of human -, I.74-7
harmonious -, IV.204
ideal -, VII.198-203
immortal -, IX.28
inner -, I.24, 67-9; II.133, 152, 175; VI.151-9
inner - and self-realization, VI.160-7
Inner - (book), I.61-106
interdependence of - within and without, VI.168-73
intoxication of -, VI.133-45
knowledge of -, VI.147-9
law of the inner -, I.85-7
law of -, VIII.150ff
-, a continual battle, VI. 77-86
- and death, VII.39-40
-, an opportunity, VI.109-17; VIII.281
- as intelligence, VIII.131, 153
- developing itself, VIII.288
- in God, III.254-5
-, interdependence of within and without, VI.168-73
- in the crowd, problem of, IX.146
- in the hereafter, VIII.175
- in the world, XI.75
- in this world, I.25ff
- is music, III.198
- of God, IX.230
- of the prophet, IX.144-7
- of sage in East, XII.106-17
- of thought, II.220-5
- phenomenon, XI.239
- power, XIII.147-9
-'s demands, VI.40
-'s journey, XI.153-7
-'s main purpose, XI.136
-'s mechanism, VIII.221-3
-'s purpose, XI.150
-'s reward, VIII.285
- today, VII.190-1
man's aim in -, XII.76ff
meaning of -, VI.145-50
mystery of -, XI.253
mysticism in -, XI.145ff
natural human -, IX.161
nature of -, VII.11; XI.229
necessity of renunciation in -, III.257
object of -, VI.16
object of the inner -, I.88-92
one -, X.131-2
ordinary -, XI.160
our -'s experience, VI.118-25
principle of -, I.150
psychology of -, I.157-8
purity of -, VI.240-5
purpose of -, I.229-31, 237-8, 240; V.192-4, 249-50; VI.24-43; VIII.135, 306; IX.11, 99, 121, 166, 213; XI.158, 238
Purpose of - (book), I.187-240
Rasa Shastra, the Science of -'s Creative Forces (book), III.115-91
realization of the inner -, I.78-81
secret of -, I.140, 156; VI.66-71
secret of human -, IX.229
silent -, II.13-16; IV.153; VII.38-45
soul as -, VIII.316-7
spiritual -, VI.152
struggle of -, VI.87-97; VIII.106-7, 227
study of -, VII.30-1; IX.165

Sufi's aim in -, IX.259ff
three aspects of -, IX.103
tragedy of -, IX.20, 115; XII.79-81
understanding of -, IX.240
what is wanted in -?, VI.72-6
worldly -, I.68-9

Light
I.27, 30-1, 44, 53, 111, 121, 135, 138, 181
II.37, 123, 149, 237, 251, 262
V.88, 91, 251
VI.121
VII.221
VIII.153, 289
IX.16, 100, 109, 110, 117, 125, 137, 143, 165, 173, 176-7, 186, 214, 216, 219, 223, 226-8, 243-4, 254-5, 268-9, 272
XI.25, 38-40, 242, 244, 256-7
all pervading -, VIII.154
celestial -, IX.258
divine -, I.28, 57, 116; V.251; VII.194; IX.97, 139, 183, 237; XI.38-40
essence of -, IX.183
faith as -, VIII.192
holiness as -, VIII.212-3
inner -, X.130
kinds of -, VIII.154
- and love, XI.50
- and Trinity, VIII.154
- as knowledge of God, VIII.13
- in our own lives, XI.39
- of Christ, IX.183
- of God, IV.71; IX.120, 140, 242; XIII.98
- of guidance, I.27
- of intelligence, I.113; II.37; VIII.153-4
- of perfection, IX.197
- of reality, XI.19
- of the abstract, II.37
- of the message, IX.228
- of the soul, VIII.303-4
- of the sun, II.37; XI.39
nature of -, VIII.184
no darkness with -, VIII.321
omnipotent -, I.113
path of -, IX.189
raising the -, XII.80
search for -, IX.63
source of -, IX.167
sphere of -, I.121
three aspects of -, XI.50-1
waves of -, XI.68

Likes
- and dislikes, XIII.71-2

Limitation(s)
I.150, 161
II.146, 163
IV.120, 230
VI.190, 196, 268
VII.188
VIII.51, 293
IX.101, 159, 165, 237
XI.167, 219, 229, 232, 234-5
XII.79-80
from - to perfection, VI.181-94
-s, IX.65

Limitlessness
ideal of -, IX.52

Line(s)
IX.191
X.160-2
- in the mind, XIII.62-7
symbolism of -, XIII.100-1

Link
sympathetic -, I.180, 182

Lion
I.101
VII.50
XI.134
quality of -, I.101
parable of the -, I.202
-s, II.26

Liquor
IX.112

Literature
XI.147

Live
desire to -, I.192-7

Living
I.222, 224

VII.50
XI.241, 248
Living Dead, The (play)
XII.195-214
Lobh
V.143
Logic
IX.168
XIII.252
Logos
I.111
III.220
London
group in -, XII.92
Loneliness
IX.83
Longing
IV.231
VI.227
IX.83
Lord
IX.114, 264
X.187
Los Angeles
University of -, XII.153
Loss
IX.98, 111
- and gain, II.79; VII.119-23
- and renunciation, III.259-60
Lot
-'s wife, IX.218-21; XIII.126-8
Love
I.13, 19, 23, 43-4, 70, 72, 99-100, 116, 138, 150, 216, 232, 239-40
II.133, 145, 237
III.99, 141
IV.156
V.17-8, 143, 146, 149, 163, 167, 169, 179, 182-3
VII.11, 13, 73, 74, 78-9, 81, 139-40, 210-11, 260
VIII.30, 96, 111, 153, 225-6, 255-60, 263-5
IX.14, 19-20, 25, 39, 57, 64, 65, 66, 95, 113-14, 137, 182, 187, 197-8, 226, 230, 239, 259, 260-1, 265
X.44-6, 134, 186
XI.60, 104, 112, 115, 131, 151, 159, 162, 164, 167, 188-91, 230, 233, 235-7, 244, 248, 252 258
XII.87
XIII.186
concentration of -, VII.78
dependent -, VII.77
divine -, V.179-87; IX.94, 216, 229
dual aspect of -, IX.114
free -, III.155
God as -, VIII.96, 111
- affairs, III.145
- as wisdom, VIII.255
- creator of beauty, VII.13
-, harmony and beauty, VII.11-20
-, human and divine, V.143; VII.73-81; VIII.285
-, *Human and Divine* (book), V.139-87
- in heart of man, VIII.262
- inherent in every soul, V.145
- in sage or holy man, VII.76
-, lover and beloved, I.24
- of Christ, IX.222, 228
- of God, I.143
- of life, I.97
- vs. law, VIII.111
magnetism of -, XI.104
manifestations of -, I.239
moral of -, V.158-70
objects of -, VII.17
pain and -, V.163; VII.13
philosophy of -, V.143-9
power of -, V.148; VII.14-5
sins against -, V.160
source of creation, V.144
unselfish -, X.100
wise -, III.149
Lover
III.135
XI.162
- and beloved, V.17; VII.14
- to Beloved, IX.35
signs of -, V.164

types of -s, III.131-3
Loyalty
I.90
Luqman
XII.83
Luminosity
I.181
Lute
IX.243
- of Orpheus, IX.217

Machine
-s, IX.92
Madani, Abu Hashim
(see Abu Hashim Madani)
Madeniat
V.25
Madzub
I.105
II.224
VII.114
VIII.63
- in Calcutta, XII.144-5
-s, 143-5, XII.143-5
story of a -, X.124
Magic
XI.115
Magician
IV.230
V.73
Magnet
IV.175
Magnetism
I.98, 174
II.112, 212
III.205
IV.22, 37, 42, 66, 112, 124, 175-9
V.145, 195, 255
VI.46, 67
VII.65, 76
VIII.276
X.187-8
XI.103-5, 112, 116, 119-22, 197
breath and -, XIII.162-3
loss of -, XI.119-21
- of beings and objects, II.212
- of feeling, XI.120
- of heart, XI.103, 112-15
- of mind, XI.103, 108-11
- of the soul, XI.116-18, 121
- of the word, XI.120
- of thought, XI.120
personal -, VII.65-72
physical -, XI.105-7
spiritual -, XI.119-22
Mahabharata
IX.241
XI.183
XIII.28
Mahachandra
VIII.74
Mahadeva
(see also Shiva)
II.45
VIII.249
X.222, 227
XII.99
Maharaja of Nepal
II.210
Maharana
- of Udaipur (story), IX.34
Mahatma
IV.184-5
VIII.28-30
Maheboob Khan
XII.154
Maheish
I.193
XI.49
Mahesh (Shiva)
XIII.101
Mahila, Queen
VIII.74
Mahtab
V.24
Maiden
ideal -, IX.159
Majesty
IX.107
Majnun, Leila and
III.173
V.171-8

VI.185
VII.219, 261
IX.23
X.175
XIII.117-20

Major
- and minor, VII.176

Makna
XIII.21

Maktul
V.198

Malak
I.115
V.113

Malakut
I.141-2
IV.198
V.25

Male
VIII.94-5
XI.51
- as aspect of God, V.33-6

Malice
XIII.238-9

Man
I.14, 44, 112, 136, 139, 153
VII.154
IX.75, 110, 111, 118, 119, 141-2, 183-5, 192, 197, 247, 251, 269
XI.155, 160, 227, 241, 248, 252
XIII.23
angel--, I.89-101
animal -, VIII.28, 157
Bogey--, The (play), XII.169-193
devil -, VIII.28, 157
divine -, VIII.28
form of -, IX.205
God -, VIII.28
heaven within -, XI.231
human -, VIII.28, 157
love in -, VII.75
-, aim of creation, VIII.36
- and eloquence, VIII.203-5
- and God, difference between, IX.112
- and "I", VIII.118-9
- as machine or engineer, VIII.164-5
- as seed of God, VIII.123-7
-, Khalif of God, IX.141
-, master of his destiny, VI.216-32
- made in image of God, IX.141
"- proposes, God disposes," IX.223
-, pulled from both sides, VIII.158
-, seed of God, V.131-7; VIII.123-7
-'s aim in life, XII.76-78
-'s being, IV.71
-'s evolution, VIII.164
-'s nature, IX.244; XI.134
-'s relationship to God, IX.109-11
mundane -, I.144
our God part and our - part, VIII.118-22
perfect -, IX.160
primitive -, VIII.128
privilege of -, VIII.116
spiritual -, IX.225; XIII.97
study of -, IX.240
universe in -, XII.47-5
Vision of God and -, The (book), XII.7-124

Mana
II.65
VI.146
VII.52
-, manu, man, IV.133
-, manu, manusha, VII.127

Manamayakosh
XIII.127

Manas
I.136
XIII.64, 181, 261

Manashni
IX.178

Manchandra
XIII.41

Manifestation

I.27, 29, 112, 133-64
II.15, 18, 106, 121, 123, 130, 140, 159, 186, 205
V.24-7, 87-99, 250
VI.88
VII.240
VIII.153
IX.103, 105, 258
X.232
XI.22, 63-4, 100, 154, 164, 169, 245, 248, 252, 256
God's nature is -, V.94
- and direction, XI.23
-, gravitation, assimilation, and perfection, VIII.153-62
- of God, IX.183
- of sound on physical plane, II.106-9
purpose of -, I.232; XI.17, 250
seven aspects of -, V.25
seven planes of -, V.24
towards -, I.113-132

Mankind
classes of -, III.132
heart of -, IX.20

Manner
VI.254
XII.69
divine -, IX.111-13, 120
- of friendliness, XIII.193-8
- of God, IX.111, 144
spiritual -, IX.175

Manners
III.110
IX.111
XI.118

Manomaya akasha
IX.219-20

Mansur al-Hallaj
(see Hallaj)

Mantiq-ut-Tayr
X.131

Mantle
IV.217
- of Muhammad, IX.194

Mantra
(see also Wazifa)
II.92, 103, 133, 167, 180
IV.250
VIII.283
XI.90
XII.118
- Shastra, II.108; IV.250

Mantra Yoga
VII.210
XI.90-1
XII.103, 118
XIII.18

Manu
VII.127
-, manushi, VII.52

Manusha
III.132
XII.41

Marathi
- poet, VII.42; XIII.249

Marefat
VII.36-7
IX.199-200
XII.36

Marriage
III.153-7
VIII.37, 251-4
IX.31, 158
XIII.27

Martyrs
IX.144

Mary
VIII.182

Mary Magdelene
VIII.182

Masnavi-i Ma'navi
II.15, 85, 187, 237
V.22
IX.151
X.127, 140, 216
XI.62

Masses
IX.162

Master(s)
I.14, 27-34, 101
II.62, 215
VI.222
VIII.249
IX.127-8, 129, 132-4, 142-3, 222, 228, 234, 267

X.101
XI.43, 246, 251
dealing with -, III.246-7
- aspect in man, VII.159
-, Saint and Prophet, IX.132-5
our dealings with -s, III.246-7
path of -, XIII.275
personality of -, IX.223, 227
qualities of -, IX.243
spiritual -, IX.166
-s, the, I.30ff
teachings of -, II.165

Mastery
I.19, 29, 52, 87, 93, 150, 158
II.33, 234
III.197
IV.119-25, 147, 151, 283
VI.99, 221, 223
VIII.43, 48, 52, 223
IX.128, 132, 147
XI.77, 83, 246
XII.82-93
XIII.31, 294-5
Ghazali on -, XII.88
- of feelings, XI.126
- of thoughts, XI.126
secret of -, IV.257

Matanat
XIII.194

Mate
right -, III.145

Materialism
I.144, 148
IX.29, 82-3, 248
XI.231
XII.56
reign of -, IX.63

Materialization
IV.150

Mathematics
study of -, III.78-9

Matr
X.212

Matter
I.163
II.17, 37, 100, 108, 148, 175
IV.39
VIII.316
IX.103
XI.22, 57-62, 63-5, 66-9, 73
spirit and -, V.27; XI.57-69

Maturity
VIII.323
IX.85

Maula Bakhsh
II.36
XII.129
death of -, XII.136

Maya
I.156, 162
VII.12, 183
VIII.189, 200
IX.224
X.170
XII.136
XIII.94, 250, 280

Meaning
- of life, VI.145

Meat
VIII.298-9
XIII.213-4

Mecca
II.202, 206
IX.170, 199, 241
X.259
pilgrimage to -, IV.54

Mechanism
VI.99
life's -, VIII.221-3
- of life, VIII.221-3
- of the universe, IX.104

Medals
loss of gold -, XII.138

Medication
II.141

Medicine(s)
IV.33, 63, 88
VIII.54, 299
XI.27
XIII.162
healing by -, IV.63-4

Medina
X.259

Meditation
I.96-7, 201-2
II.169, 233, 248

IV.122, 155, 167, 172, 206, 236
VI.69, 143, 274
VII.42, 197
VIII.133, 320
XI.69, 122, 190, 200
X.27
XII.83, 102
breathing and -, XIII.161
path of -, XII.23-8

Medium
I.14, 170
X.121

Meekness
IX.189, 203
X.204

Mehrab
XII.94

Memory
II.231
III.78
IV.136, 154, 252
VIII.197
XI.108-9
XIII.220

Men
our dealings with fellow--, III.249-50

Mental
reproduction of - record, XIII.62-3

Mentality
XI.78, 243

Mercy
I.58, 60
II.28
V.24, 207
VIII.121
IX.42, 94, 104, 189

Merit
IX.88
-s, IX.102-3; XI.198-9

Mesquin
XII.141

Message
I.32-3
VI.122, 138
VIII.20, 37-8
IX.18, 125, 128, 129, 130, 134, 143, 145, 151, 173, 190, 225, 227-8, 233-47, 249, 269-270
assimilating the -, IX.245-6
divine -, I.14, 15, 101, 118; IX.16, 81, 119, 136, 146, 217, 240, 253-4
divine --bearer, I.14
following the -, IX.145
fulfillment of -, IX.148
God's -, XI.253
light of the -, IX.228, 246
- and messenger, IX.233-46
--bearer(s), IX.136, 151
- of God, I.15; VII.178; IX.125-6, 148, 186, 226
- of the day, IX.20, 138
- to humanity, X.93
Muhammad's -, IX.230
receiving the -, IX.245-6
representing the -, IX.245-6
spiritual -, IX.150
Sufi -, IX.148, 247-51, 262, 269
Sufi - of Spiritual Liberty (book), V.9-36

Messenger(s)
I.29
II.51
VII.228
VIII.35, 37-8, 190
IX.16, 30, 117-8, 119, 125, 136, 139, 220-1, 222-7, 233-46
X.121
XII.132
five aspects of -, IX.242
friend of the -, IX.235
- of God, IX.241
presence of -, IX.241, 245
secret of -, IX.238
spirit of -, IX.240
what is asked of -, IX.243
world -, IX.130-1

Messiah
IV.85

Metaphysics

X.93
XI.158
XIII.241-296
- (book), V.225-56
Method
Sufi -, IV.254, 256
Microbes
IV.24
Middle age
IX.56
Middle Ages
X.205
art of --, X.175-6
Mildness
VII.68
Milk
IX.201
Mind
I.102, 124-6, 136, 139, 153-160, 167-8, 177-8, 201
II.44, 59, 60, 107, 110, 226, 232, 259
III.20, 170
IV.99, 103-6, 134, 160, 169, 191, 196, 200, 210, 225, 241, 252
V.42, 45, 84. 215, 235, 242-3
VI.14, 20, 146
VII.52-6, 63, 104, 124-30, 173, 237
VIII.176
IX.100, 139, 220, 237-8, 240
X.21, 40
XI.41, 59, 123, 127-8, 197, 229-30, 242, 247, 253
XII.60, 86
XIII.51, 60, 261-2
activity of -, VII.124-5; XIII.70-1
awakening the -, IX.176
body of -, IV.192; IX.219
breath and - , VII.103
breath in development of -, XIII.153-4
clear -, XI.110
constitution of -, V.234-5
control of -, IV.132-47
cultivation of -, II.79
different aspects of -, I.158
different qualities of -, XIII.60-1
divine -, VII.54; IX.130, 139; XI.212
effect of food on -, IX.200-1
faculties of the -, VI.79
five aspects of -, IV.135
five faculties of -, V.235
five qualities of -, I.201
human and divine -, VII.52-6
impressions on -, XIII.227-8
inequality of -, VII.173
influence of - on body, V.235-6
inspired -, VIII.268
keeping - pure, XIII.228-31
language of the -, XIII.66-7
living -, XI.110
magnetism of -, XI.108
master--, VI.221; VII.153-61
master of -, I.93
mechanism of -, X.49
- and body, V.110; XII.16
- and brain, VII.52
- and heart, II.251ff; IV.246
--body conection, I.159
-, human and divine, VII.52ff
- is storehouse, IV.105
- (mental world), I.125-6
- of infant, III.24
--*world, The* (book), IV.239-288
normal state of -, XI.77
philosophical -, I.103
power of -, IV.77-8; XIII.225-6
pure -, IV.103-7
purification of -, XIII.223-5, 239
purifying the -, IV.100
purify - from fear, XIII.237-8
purity of -, IV.73; XIII.221-23
rhythm of -, XI.31
standards of -, XIII.226-7
stilling the -, VI.14; VII.124-31
strength of -, III.106; VI.254

subconscious -, IV.106
training of the -, VII.126; VIII.43
Mineral kingdom
I.28, 111, 135
VIII.288
IX.39
qualities of -, I.90; XI.155
Minor
- and major, VII.176
Miracle(s)
IX.51-2, 180-1
XIII.259
Mirage
XI.35
Miraj
VII.52
-, the dream of the prophet, IX.230
Miran Datar
II.206
V.75
Mirror(s)
I.149, 159
III.211
IV.241, 246, 263
VIII.162, 315
IX.112
looking in -, III.73
- and rust, IV.264
palace of -s, IV.241
Mirth
II.28
Misery
IV.111
XII.47
cause of -, XII.47
Misfortune
IV.111
Misra
II.45
Mission
I.193
V.20
Mistakes
VI.255
XI.196
Mithal
V.68
Mithea
IX.224
Mithya
XIII.94
Mitra
X.212
Mlench
XII.134
Modernism
IX.29
Modesty
III.138-41
IX.224
XI.81, 135
XIII.199-201
Moin-ud-Din Chishti, Khwaja
II.60, 98, 203
V.22, 32, 119
X.66
Moghul
X.204
Mohammed
(see Muhammed)
Mohammedans
(see also Muslims)
XIII.23
Mohammad Shah
X.224
Moin-ud-Din Chishti, Khwaja
tomb of -, XII.140
Moksha
VII.206
IX.260
Monday
XIII.42
Money
I.219
II.176
VII.247
XII.52
pursuit of -, IX.12
Mongolian
X.203
Monkey
VIII.236
three -s, IV.236
Monogamy

III.170-3

Monotheism
IX.67-9, 275-6

Moon
III.124
IX.20, 125
X.215
XI.39
magnetism of -, XI.104
- balancing sun, III.123-4

Moral(s)
I.19, 57-60, 84
VIII.200
IX.76-7, 102, 191
XIII.167-203
- conception, IX.277
- *Culture* (book), III.229-62
- hallucination, I.23
- law, I.85
- principle, IX.267
- principles, I.97
Sufi -, IX.265
three stages of -, III.255

Mortality
I.19, 156-7, 166, 193-4
V.253
VI.19, 273
IX.221
X.16
XI.249, 257
- in East, XII.160-1

Moses
I.33
II.26, 62, 75, 242, 261
IV.76
V.185
VII.25, 137
VIII.37
IX.144, 147, 173-4, 179, 186, 198, 208, 241, 258, 270, 271-2
X.67, 154
XI.166, 179
XII.133
- and Khizr. IX.105
- on Mt. Sinai, VII.41
- walking in wilderness, IX.173
story of boy, V.185
story of God's visit, x183

Mosques
IX.215

Mother
III.14, 122
V.36, 118, 147
IX.181
X.63
compassion of -, XI.188
responsibility of - toward child, V.35
role of -, V.35

Moti Mahal
X.204

Motive
I.162
III.156
IV.158
VI.177, 235
IX.259
X.195
XI.187, 242
- of soul, IX.192

Motubah
XIII.194

Mourning
IV.247
V.196
IX.189

Movement(s)
II.73, 123
III.62
IV.22
IX.115, 222, 273
XI.93, 106
XIII.57-8
art of -, XI.94
controlling -, XI.93
kinds of -, XI.92
life is -, IV.22
psychology of -, XI.93
refined -, XI.93
repressed -, XI.93
significance of -, XI.94
Sufi -, IX.249, 252, 255, 262-3, 267-70
suggestion by -, XI.92

Mozart

X.231
Muezzin
call of the -, IX.196
Muhammad, the Prophet
I.33
II.26, 36, 41, 46, 62, 65, 175
III.51, 122
VI.31, 62, 162
VII.25, 117
VIII.13, 172, 289
IX.30, 106, 125, 144, 147, 150, 170, 179, 193-203, 208, 240, 244, 247, 258, 264, 270, 277
X.16, 64, 67, 93, 96, 99, 101, 102, 109, 140, 253, 258
XI.166
XII.57, 133-4, 141
XIII.22, 28, 194
breast of -, IX.193
command to -, IX.194
contemplation of -, IX.194
"Die before death...", I.195
"Every person is...", IX.53
"Every soul...", IX.15
faith of -, VII.92-3
final initiation of -, XIII.122
"God is beautiful", I.20; VII.12; XI.192
guidance of -, IX.194
"I am knowledge...", IX.145
"I am wisdom...", IX.244
"I existed...", I.34
manner of -, VIII.264-5
mantle of -, IX.194
marriage of -, IX.194
Meraj of -, VII.52; XIII.108, 121-2
message of -, IX.195, 230
"My child...", I.215
- and dates, IV.92
- and resignation, VIII.70
- and slave, VII.175
- fulfilled mission, V.20
- on balance, VIII.63
- on brotherhood, VII.165
- on death, XIII.104
- on marriage, III.178-80
- on virtue, III.213
"One will have...", I.158
opening breast of -, XIII.120
responsibility of -, IX.193
saying of -, VIII.324
"This life...", I.159
"Tie your camel", VII.247; IX.106, XIII.265
youth of -, IX.193-5
Mukhya
II.54
Mukti
II.139, 151
VIII.166, 168, 172, 312
X.125
Mummies
XIII. 40
Muni
VIII.102, 206
X.76
Munkir
I.121
- and Nakir, V.52
Mureeds
IX.190
Murshid
I.14, 48, 52, 76, 95
II.159, 170, 244
IV.93
V.221-4, 248
VI.76, 165-6
VIII.209, 244
IX.170, 190
X.109
XI.214
XII.73, 115, 162
XIII.198
kinds of -, V.221
- and mureed, V.24; XII.94
- and notebook, II.233
- of murshids, IX.188
-s, IV.93
Muruat
VIII.237-8
XII.94
Muse ke
II.75
Musheraff Khan

XII.154
Mushroom
XIII.102-3
Music
I.26, 41-2, 116, 180, 194
II.27, 44, 50-61, 73, 78, 86, 98, 104, 108, 115, 122, 135, 143, 149, 191, 204, 218
III.27, 88, 226
V.31
VI.131
IX.48-9, 254
X.127, 221-29, 259
XI.32, 35, 147
ancient -, II.89-95
celestial -, IX.146
composition of -, II.55
five aspects of -, V.31
healing power of -, II.141
Hindu forms of -, II.45, 53, 96, 105
instruction in -, II.101, 104
instrumental -, II.56, 63, 92, 103, 110
man is -, life is -, IV.21
- among Sufis, V.31-2
- as meditation, II.77
- as one life, VIII.134
- (book), II.69-152
- of life, IV.19; VIII.104, 134
- of the spheres, II.7, 78-88, 173
organ -, II.111
periods of Indian -, II.98
pitch in -, II.114
psychic influence of -, II.135-40
scales in -, II.98
science and art of Hindu -, II.96-102
scientific aspects of -, II,90, 96
silent -, XIII.82-3
spiritual development by aid of -, II.147-52
technique in -, II.55
vocal -, II.55, 145
Musician
II.53, 104, 136
IX.115
XI.212
Muslim(s)
I.54
VII.165
VIII.212
IX.148, 258
X.140, 257
XI.164
Muss
V.26
Mussolini
IV.164
Mussulmans
(see also Muslims)
XIII.21
Mutmaina
V.25
XI.202
XII.34
XIII.181
Mutu kubla anta mutu
V.47
Muwakkals (elementals)
II.18, 106, 222
Mysteries
Greek -, XIII.29-32
- of life, IX.214
Mystery
I.138
III.203
IX.249
X.17
Mystic
I.56, 104
II.161
IV.45, 120, 194, 256
V.212
VI.124, 277
VII.54, 55, 226, 230, 242
VIII.118, 137, 195, 289, 207
IX.36, 145, 191, 224, 230
X.13-9, 20-6, 28-35, 50, 53, 73, 126, 145, 251, 258
XI.59, 146-8, 150-1, 158-60, 169-70, 173, 178, 181, 186, 196, 200, 205, 210, 215, 221-2, 227, 241, 254

XII.20, 64, 83, 93
dream of -, XI.217
ideal of -, XI.166-8
inspiration and power of -, XI.220-3
joke of -, XI.220
judging a -, XI.222
knowledge of -, X.24-5
language of -, XI.150-1
meditation of -, XI.219
moral of -, XI.151, 179-82
- and scientist, XII.82
- eye, XI.213
- idea of faith, VII.87
- point of view, X.20-1
- relaxation, IV.162-74
-'s nature, XI.215-9
nature and work of -, X.30-5
outlook of -, X.23; XI.218-9
path of -, XI.204
power of -, XI.221
pursuit of -, XI.204
question of -, XI.212-4
realization of -, XI.219
religion of -, XI.151
sign of -, XI.227
simplicity of -, X.25-6
striving of -, XI.158
temperament of -, XI.216-7
vision of -, X.24; XI.210-14

Mystical
- outlook, XI.186

Mysticism
I.56, 104
II.59, 121, 151, 185
IV.120
VI.24
IX.170, 218
X.13-9
XI.74, 87, 150, 183, 186, 192
XII.20-2, 64, 162-3
definition of -, XI.151
Hebrew -, IX.258
- (book), XI.143ff
- in life, XI.145-9
- of breath, XIII.143-4
- *of Sound* (book), II.9-67
secret of -, I.159; IV.203
Sufi - (book), X.9ff
way to learn -, XI.150

Myth
IX.206, 224
- of Balder, XIII.110-11

Nabi
I.29
V.25
IX.128, 130, 136
XI.216

Nabitat
V.25

Nada
II.97
VIII.154
X.222
XI.58

Nada Brahma
II.39, 157, 185
IV.79
VII.210
XI.58
XII.118

Nafs
(see also Ego)
I.39, 121
II.26, 31, 32
IV.189
VI.87
VII.251, 269
VIII.52, 185-7
X.86
XI.131, 201
XII.90
XIII.137, 173
--e-Ammara, III.166
--e-Lawwama, III.166
--e-Mutmaina, III.167
--e-Salima, III.167

Nafsi Garm
XIII.159-60

Nafs-Kushi
V.195
VII.270

Naghat

V.26
Nahazat
I.167
Najat
VIII.172, 210
V.11
XII.140
Nakhra (radiance)
III.151-2
Nakir
I.121
Nakshi Bandi
XIII.89-131
Name
I.121
II.33, 163, 174
IX.88, 101
XI.87
meaning of -, II.34
mystery hidden in -, II.33
- of God, IX.113, 138
-s, XI.89-90
-s of God, I.42, 91; IX.52, 101, 258
sacred - of God, II.35, 157
Names and forms
XIII.250, 252
Naminaust
VI.88
Nanak
V.253
VIII.144
XII.152
"The grains...", IX.53
Napoleon
IV.165
VII.139
XI.80
- on Josephine, III.126
Naqshaband
(see Baha-ud-Din)
Naqshi
V.29
Naqshibandi
VIII.18
Nar
I.121
V.91
Narada
II.75, 115
X.227
Narayana
XIII.142
Nari
V.91
Narrowness
IX.112
Nasut
I.141-2
IV.198
V.25
Nation
IX.205
desire of -s, VII.162-9
Nationalism
I.18
VII.177
Natural
XI.185
Nature
I.15
II.55, 80, 86, 133, 179, 189, 202, 222
V.12, 90, 200
VI.74, 83, 182
VII.25, 204
VIII.246
IX.48-50, 78, 92, 102, 103, 125, 173, 175, 190, 194, 196, 267
X.168
XI.41, 49-52, 134, 137, 169-72, 185, 192-3, 251
- and art, XII.33
- and character, XI.134-41
divine -, IX.16, 51, 103
dual aspect of -, XI.51
help of -, X.93
human -, I.223; IX.112, 116, 165, 205, 223, 253
laws of -, IX.200
man's -, IX.244
-'s religion, VII.21-31
mechanism of -, VII.38
spiritual circulation through veins of -, VIII.131-5

tendency to rise in -, VII.214
threefold, dual and unique aspects of -, XI.49-52
unique character of -, XI.52

Natures
V.25

Nayat
XIII.31

Nayaz
III.151

Naz
III.151

Naza
I.167
VIII.173

Nazar
I.163

Nazar ba kadam
XII.141
XIII.152

Nazr
XIII.182

Nearness
- to Creator, IX.129
- to God, IX.35

Need
IX.46

Negative
- and positive, XII.40

Neighbours
our dealings with -, III.248-9

Nepal
IV.143
X.193
meeting a muni in -, XII.139

Nerves
III.32, 200
IV.35, 38, 50
VI.100

Nervous system
XIII.162

New Testament
IX.150

New York
X.220
XII.49

Newspaper
XII.49

Nickname
II.36

Nida
V.32

Night
IX.219

Niman
VIII.63

Nimaz
IX.202-3
XII.130

Nirva
IX.38

Nirvana
II.77, 139, 151, 250
IV.166
V.121
VI.121
VII.182
VIII.42, 48, 166, 312
X.23, 125
XI.245, 250

Nizam of Hyderabad
I.210
VI.87, 228
VII.99
VIII.261
XII.93, 137
XIII.202
"You look at me...", I.237

Nizami
VIII.14

Nizam-ud-Din
V.22, 74

Nizam-ud-Din Wali, Khwaja
V.74

Noah
VII.228

Nobility
I.220
VIII.239
IX.74

Nobleness
III.222

Noisiness
III.207

Normal
- and abnormal, IV.285

North Pole
IX.219
Note
divine -, IX.111
Nothing
XI.248
-ness, II.262; VIII.102
Now
IV.268
Nur
I.111-2, 117, 121, 128, 152
IV.76
V.25, 43, 91
XII.13
Nur-e Mohammad
I.27
Nur-i Jehan
X.204
Nursing
- infants, III.19-20, 30
Nur-Zahur
I.27-30, 111, 117
Nrutya, Lassia and Tandeva
II.45
Numbers
unlucky -, XIII.43-4
Numerology
II.35
Nuzul
V.14
- and Uruj, V.26

Object
X.121
XI.40-1, 97
XII.48
life in -s, VII.38
magnetism of beings and -s, II.212
- of inner life, I.88-92
- of journey, I.70-3
- of praise, I.20
-s of Sufi Movement, IX.267-8
Obligation(s)
IX.97
XI.247
fulfillment of -, I.74-7
Obscurity
IX.167
Observation
X.108
XII.66
Obsession
I.174
IV.30, 247
V.72-7
Occultism
XI.149
XII.27
Ocean
VIII.160, 169-70, 278
IX.119
- in drop, XIII.91-2
Pearls from the - Unseen (book), V.189-223
Offerings
IV.247
freewill -, IX.156
Oil
IX.226-7
Old Testament
IX.150, 173
X.215
Om
II.66
Omar, Khalif of Arabia
II.82
Omar Khayyam
I.229
II.232
III.261
IV.170
VII.152, 156
X.94, 130
XII.143
Omega
(see Alpha and Omega)
XI.167
Omen(s)
XI.85
mysteries of -, XIII.44-5
Omnipotent
- light, I.113
Omniscient

IV.123
IX.112
One
IX.101, 103, 105, 107, 114, 202, 247
- and two, XI.44-5
perfect -, I.172
pure -, IX.92
Oneness
I.18, 237
IV.252
V.103
VII.53-4
VIII.100, 135
IX.84, 79, 88, 228, 236, 266
XII.27
Absolute -, XIII.54
- of God, IX.196
Openness
IX.229
XIII.56-7, 80-1
Opinion(s)
II.150
XI.78
XII.29
XIII.276-8
Opportunity
I.228
IX.227
life an -, VI.109-17; XIII.131
Opposite(s)
VIII.45, 130, 311
XI.51, 176
attraction of -, VIII.94-5
- of God, VIII.97
- point of view, X.21
pairs of -s, VIII.97-103
to distinguish by -s, VIII.129
Opposition
I.25
IX.108
XII.92
Optimism
I.178, 183
VI.81
VII.229
VIII.245-6, 286, 306
XI.100
- and pessimism, VIII.245-6
Optimist
I.178
Oracle
-s, XIII.28
Order
IX.130
Organ
XI.29
generative -s, III.181
nature of senses and their -s, V.231-2
Origin
I.172
Orphans
III.51
Orpheus
II.54, 75, 163
VIII.190-3
XIII.123
lute of -, IX.217
Orthodoxy
IX.148
XI.161, 166
idea of faith in -, VII.87
religious ideal of -, XI.166
Othello
VII.88-9
XIII.201
Others
dealings of -, III.238-9, 241-
sharing with -, XIII.198-9
Outlook
VIII.248
X.92
XI.147
Overlooking
VII.257
VIII.241-2

Pacifism
IX.254
Paderewski
IV.153
XIII.282
Padmani

III.135
IX.148

Pain
IV.62-3
VI.122
VIII.72, 137, 269, 319
IX.95, 115, 216-7, 223-5
X.209
XI.229

Painting
X.180-5

Pala
I.115

Palestine
IX.148
X.253

Pandava
IX.162

Pani
XIII.149

Pantheism
IX.68-9, 275-6

Paradise
I.127, 167-8, 227
IX.260
XI.189

Paramatma
IV.184, 186
VIII.28, 31

Parenting
IX.31

Parents
I.29
III.51, 104-5
V.115
VII.116
XI.135
influence of -, VII.116
inheritance from -, IV.275-6

Paris
XII.155

Parsis
IX.146, 177, 258
X.80, 120
XIII.21, 23

Part
our God - and our man -, VIII.118
playing a -, XI.249

Parvati
II.45, 104
IX.207

Pasi Anfas
XIII.133-64

Passion(s)
III.162-4
IV.36
XI.190, 229
-s of the senses, III.163
sex -, III.164-5

Passive
- and active, VIII.68, 72

Passivity
I.68
IV.122
VI.166
VIII.72

Past
X.33
forgetting the -, VII.46
knowledge of -, present and future, VII.145ff
re-echo of -, XIII.79-80

Pataloka
VIII.321

Path
I.21, 235
VII.156, 262
IX.188, 267
XI.135, 149
different steps on -, X.82-6
four -s which lead to the goal, VII.262-6
inner -, X.48
intellectual -, VII.262
- of attainment, VI.195-206
- of devotion, VII.265-6
- of discipline, VII.263-5
- of goodness, IX.178
- of initiation, X.61-70
- *of Initiation and Discipleship* (book), X.57-114
- of meditation, XII.23-8
- of righteousness, VII.263
- to God, XI.161
prophetic -, key to, IX.151

spiritual -, I.189; IX.96, 101-2, 255; XI.166, 205
spiritual -, advancement on, IX.50
stages on - of self-realization, VI.207-15
steps on -, X.85
what is needed on -, X.78-81

Patience
I.97
III.31, 63
VII.49, 76-7
VIII.52-3, 71, 85, 171, 240, 243, 275
IX.95, 107, 134, 246, 253
X.79
XI.91, 115, 163, 211, 253
XII.20
XIII.247-9
-in guardian, III.31

Patr
X.212

Payghambar
I.33
IX.136
X.121

Peace
I.58, 209-12
II.17, 235, 259
VI.22, 29, 77, 115
VII.30
VIII.218, 272, 274
IX.31, 130, 190, 195, 248-9, 254, 266
X.113, 244
XI.203, 243, 244
inner -, VI.22
message of -, IX.247
- and order, lack of, IX.33
temple of -, IX.230

Peaches
Chinese symbolof -, XIII.105

Peacock
- feathers, IV.91; IX.217; XIII.123

Pearls
- *from the Ocean Unseen* (book), V.189-256

People
two classes of -, V.192

Perception
I.150
XI.42, 103, 108-9, 196, 257
XII.61
inner -, five centers of, I.150

Perfection
I.21, 24, 29, 67, 69, 91-2, 95, 145, 172, 225-8
II.102, 136, 151, 186-8
III.154
IV.120, 121
V.18-9, 99, 101
VI.123, 181, 183, 190, 194, 214, 237
VII.219
VIII.21, 26, 102, 157, 168, 177, 187, 252, 304
IX.23, 46, 51, 65, 70-1, 74, 81, 84, 85, 90-2, 98-9, 110, 113, 114, 119, 135, 142, 161, 175, 181-2, 191, 203, 218, 237, 249, 257, 267
X.19
XI.84, 133, 182, 219-20, 250, 253
XII.50, 75
claim of -, IX.242
consciousness of -, I.232
divine -, I.237
from limitation to -, VI.181-94
human -, III.122
ideal of -, VIII.18
light of -, IX.197
manifestation, gravitation, assimilation, and -, VIII.153-62
path of -, VIII.213
- of God, IX.101, 120
spiritual -, IX.102, 250

Peri
green -, VII.80
-s, V.162
-s, VII.80

Perplexity
IX.139

Perseverance

XI.91, 102
Persia
VIII.14
IX.48, 176, 252
X.111, 123, 126, 129-31, 147, 151, 182, 203-4, 216-8, 253
Persian(s)
VIII.169, 208, 251
X.123, 126, 147-8, 151, 198, 204, 21, 225, 227
XIII.16, 28
- literature, XIII.108
- poets, X.126-30
Person
III.214
spiritual -, IX.161
two types of -s, III.218
Personality, -ies
I.137
III.214
IV.272-3, 283
VI.44, 54, 75
VII.32, 117
VIII.239, 261, 267-9, 280, 295
IX.70, 139, 166, 222, 225
XI.59, 78, 118, 134, 138, 140-1, 156-7, 163-4, 177, 228, 237, 251-2, 256, 258
XII.33
art of -, III.214-28; VI.44-51; X.166; XI.251-2; XIII.193
art of - like music, III.227
Character-Building and the Art of - (book), III.193-228
development of -, VI.52-9; X.143; XII.33-7; XIII.169-73
divine -, IX.89, 112
God-realized -, IX.182
human -, IX.86, 89, 118, 179, 249
idea of -, IX.204
learning art of -, III.214-5
- of God, VII.32-7
- of Master, IX.223, 227
spiritual -, XI.122
Persuasion
(persuasive tendency), III.219
Perversion
III.181-7
causes of -, III.182
Pessimism
I.183
VI.81
VIII.245-6, 286
XI.100
optimism and -, VIII.245-6
Pessimist
I.178
Peter
VII.92
XIII.129
Pharaoh
IX.241
Phenomena
IV.257, 275
XII.124
Philosopher
X.30-1
-'s stone, VI.12-3; IX.118
Philosophy
IX.218
X.31, 186
XI.145, 158, 232
- (book), XI.11-69
- in East, XII.161-2
- of love, V.143-9
- of resurrection, V.219-21
- of sacrament, IX.187-8
- of soul, V.83-6
Phoenix
IX.85
Physical
the -, IV.126
Physician
II.131, 141, 143, 189
ancient -s, XI.53
Physiognomy
XIII.55
Picture
symbolical -s, XII.19
Piety
XIII.265-6
Pig
IX.201
Pigeon
IX.225

Pilgrimage
I.43
II.202
IX.198
Pingala
XIII.95
Pir
IX.128, 129
XI.217
Pir-o-Murshid
I.47
X.85
- of dervishes, XII.141
Pitch
III.91
IX.111, 120
Pity
III.198
Plan
IV.227
VIII.138
X.20
Plane(s)
I.136
VII.124, 146
VIII.154-62, 179, 321-2
XI.26, 31, 37, 47, 54
physical -, VII.241
Planet(s)
I.30
II.91
IV.162
VIII.138, 142
IX.125
XI.41, 54
influence of -, VIII.142; XIII.46
intelligence of -, XI.41-2
Plans
X.23
Plant
IX.118
-s, XI.63
Plato
IV.114
VIII.22
Plays
Four - (book), XII.165-274
Pleasure
I.208
IV.161
VI.69, 135
IX.258
XI.197, 232, 258
- of God, IX.108
-s of life, VII.108
Poet
X.120
XI.188
- and prophet, X.119-22
Persian -s, X.126-30
Sufi -ic imagery, X.123-5
Sufi -s, XII.94
Poetry
I.217
II.44, 52, 217, 249
IX.49
X.119, 121, 123, 127, 130, 207-21
inspirational -, X.130
Sufi - (book), X.115-54
Point of view
IV.109
VI.64, 274
VIII.42, 62, 243, 251, 303
X.73
XI.134
artistic -, XI.106
Poison
IV.288
IX.229
bowl of -, IX.218
Poles
- of the world, IX.219
Politeness
VII.66
VIII.240
XI.137
Politics
IX.32
Polygamy
III.170, 174-80
Poor
"Blessed are the - in spirit", V.194-6; IX.189
Pork

why - prohibited, XIII.213
Positive
- and negative, III.123; XII.40
Possession
IV.121
V.13
IX.112, 172
Posture
IV.100
Postures
VII.63
XII.66
Poverty
VII.100
IX.165, 249
XII.79
Power
I.23, 67, 162, 173, 203, 226
II.236
IV.34, 77, 79, 145, 171, 180-2
VI.21, 28, 67, 85, 101, 201, 205
VII.74, 117
VIII.52, 68, 86, 306
IX.120, 125, 134, 143, 159, 204, 268
X.112
XII.64, 84
almighty -, I.176, 204
attainment of -, VII.139-41
desire for -, I.203-5
development of healing -, IV.72-9
magnetic -, IV.65
negative and positive -, III.123-4
nervous -, IV.36
- in love, VII.74, 78
- of breath, IV.74
- of character, VII.117
- of finger-tips, IV.76
- of God, IX.48
- of mind, XIII.225-6
- of mystics, XI.188
-s, use of, VII.230-1
- within us, IV.180-7
real - in feeling, IV.145
sending - to a distance, IV.79
Practice
I.158
IX.121
-s, VI.104; XI.121
suggestion in -, XI.96
Praise
IX.48-9, 239, 273
object of -, IX.267
- of God, V.214; IX.37-8, 48
Prakrit
X.214, 216-7
Prakriti
II.130
VII.12
IX.102
Pralaya
I.114
Prana
I.127-8
II.110, 135, 143
IV.15, 66
XIII.16, 137-8, 161
Pranam
IX.155
Pranamayakosh
IX.219, 221
XIII.127
Prayer(s)
III.238
IV.86, 128, 255
V.205-9
VII.99
VIII.25, 85
IX.28, 34-52, 64-5, 102, 110, 114-5, 196, 202-3, 272-3
VIII.85
XI.242, 251, 258
XII.76
effect of -, VII.98-101
five aspects of -, IX.34-6
healing by -, IV.86
house of -. IX.64
need for -, IX.36
outer form of -, IX.36
-ful attitude, V.204-6; IX.37
repetition of -, IX.51
three kinds who offer -, IX.39-40

Precautions
III.236
Predictions
II.19
Prejudice
VII.11-2
IX.63
XI.124
Preparation
- for the journey, I.65-9
Presence
IX.227, 245
Divine -, II.95; XII.68-75
healing by -, IV.85
inner - of teacher, XII.103
power of -, IV.77
- of God, I.72; VII.212-20; IX.199, 266
- of healer, IV.77
- of messenger, IX.241, 245
- of the prophet, IX.139, 146
Present
knowledge of past, - and future, VII.145-8
- re-echo of past, XIII.79
Prestara
II.98
Price
I.76
Pride
III.57, 238
VII.15
IX.34, 100
XI.99-100, 158-60, 227, 243
XIII.201
- in child, III.57
- of birth and rank, III.128
Principle
IX.102
XI.137, 174-5, 235-6
XII.45
making use of -, XI.99
-s, III.126; V.31
Prison
XIII.147
- of renunciation, VIII.75
Privilege
IX.227
- of being human, VIII.113-17
Problem
- of the day, IX.249
- *of the Day* (book), X.237-70
-s, I.211
Profit
I.17
XII.58
Progress
VII.179
IX.11, 14, 16, 54-5, 100
X.110
XII.55
human and divine -, IV.122
- of high initiates, IX.128
- of humanity, IX.230
- on the spiritual path, II.120
spiritual -, X.8
Promise
breach of -, III.156
Pronouns
personal -, IX.50
Property
IX.31
Prophecy
IX.139
X.119
seal of -, IX.128
spirit of -, I.34-8; IX.127
Prophet
I.15, 33, 101, 118, 127
VI.223, 234
IX.129, 132, 134-5, 136-8, 144-51, 228, 243
XI.125, 132, 169, 254
breast of the -, IX.228-30
dream of the -, IX.230
heart of -, IX.145-6
life of -, IX.144-7
master, saint and -, IX.132-5
mission of the -, IX.148
missions of -s, IX.79-80
path of -, key to, IX.151
poet and -, X.119-22
presence of -, IX.137, 139, 146
proof of real -, IX.195
-ic soul, IX.144

-ic tendency, I.32; IV.118; V.19, 55, 119; VII.41, 71; VIII.32-8; IX.128, 134-47, 150, 236-7, 243; X.69, 122; XI.254, 258
-s, I.31, 86; V.19-21; IX.117-8, 139, 149, 166, 186, 237, 240
-s of Beni Israel, IX.208
soul of -, IX.141
task of the -, IX.150
teachings of the -s, IX.180, 258
temperament of -, XIII.276
the -, IX.136-8
words of the -, IX.147, 151
work of the -, IX.138

Prophethood
claim of -, IX.138
proof of -, IX.138

Prophetic
- cycles, IX.51
- tendency, VIII.32-8

Propkar
VI.92

Proportion
XI.105

Proserpina
XIII.30

Prostitution
III.188-91

Prostration
IX.37, 155, 197, 216

Protection
IX.130

Protestant(ism)
IX.36, 257
- church, XI.236

Providence
VI.32
VII.245
IX.93, 102

Psalms
XII.119

Psychic powers
VII.66
IX.14

Psychoanalysis
II.144
IX.166

Psychology
I.157
II.135, 167
VI.153
XI.73-4, 123, 145
- (book), XI.73-141
-, master of mind, XI.123-8
- of crowd, XI.75
- of shadow, XIII.33-4
science and -, XI.73-4
Sufi -, XII.38-41

Puja
IX.215-6
XIII.113

Pungi
II.54, 110

Punishment
III.47
V.210
VIII.94, 167, 202

Pulserat
V.59

Pupil
IX.128
X.88
how to be a -, II.150

Puranas
X.214

Puran Bhagat
VII.74

Pure
IX.200
- One, IX.92

Purgatory
I.167
V.59, 105

Purification
II.16, 83
IV.72-3, 99,102, 286
IX.176, 215
XI.258
XIII.113, 121, 139, 216-7, 220-1, 228-9
Mental - (book), IV.95-237
- of the heart, IX.229, 258
- of mind, XIII.223-5
real - of mind, XIII.239

Purity
I.161, 182
VI.240-5
VII.56
IX.28, 112, 189, 253, 256-7
XI.238
XII.29, 32
XIII.209-10, 218, 265
- of body, XIII.219-20
- of heart, XIII.232-3, 236, 239
- of life, VI.240-5
- of mind, IV.73; XIII. 221-225
Purpose
I.16, 23, 26, 47, 58, 112, 133, 140, 144-5, 163, 184, 189, 234
II.151, 223, 238
III.22
IV.119
V.193, 249
VI.24, 31, 34, 36, 42, 123
VII.163
VIII.87, 127, 157
IX.68, 71, 76, 103, 110, 121, 159, 179, 220, 253, 267
X.22-3, 100, 143, 145-6, 252
XI.141, 235, 237
- of creation, IX.175, 177, 192
- of life, I.23-4, 229-31, 237-8, 240; V.192-4, 249-50; VI.24-43; VII.89; IX.91-2, 99, 213; XI.245
- *of Life* (book), I.187-240
- of Sufi Movement, IX.270-3
- of whole creation, XI.245
Sufi -, I.13
Purusha
II.66, 130
VII.12
IX.102
Putra
II.53
Pyramids
X.202
Qadiri
VIII.18
Qalbi
V.29
Qasab-e Kousein
X.204
Qawwali
I.41-3
V.32
XIII.31
Qayamat
V.60-1
Qoniya (Konya)
XII.74
Qualities
III.71
VIII.94, 157-8
IX.102
XII.89
inherited -, III.13-14; IV.275
heart -, IX.258
Quality
attraction of -, XII.40
Question(s)
I.235
XI.129, 212, 214, 227, 231, 249, 258
answer in every -, VIII.130
answer to every -, IX.82
- of mystic, XI.212-4
- why?, VIII.130
Quietism
I.77
VIII.18
Qul
V.32
Qur'an
I.85, 141, 156, 204, 207
II.237
III.29, 237, 249, 254
IV.242, 252
V.12, 19, 44, 56, 58, 59, 122, 131, 183, 195, 208, 220
VI.64, 66, 78, 120, 170, 227, 268
VII.36, 55, 77, 85, 187
VIII.116, 145, 153-4, 203, 228, 289

IX.38, 48, 114, 146, 183, 196, 258
X.130, 262
XI.24, 57, 169, 217
XII.52, 85, 131, 149, 160, 162
XIII.31, 59, 93, 249
"Allah loves the patient", VII.77
"...angels knew nothing...", I.115
"Be! He said...", I.156
"By the night...", IX.196
creation of man in -, VII.85
"Die before death", VII.187; VIII.228
"Cry aloud the Name...", IX.194, 196
"God created the world...", IX.223
"God is all...", VIII.145
"God is free...", I.141
God is light, VII.263
God is rich, VII.99; XII.79
"He who taught...", I.85; VII.145
"I have made...", VIII.154
"If we had not...", IX.38
"Mutu kubla...", VII.187; VIII.228
"O Lord, bless this...", IX.198
"Say who...",IX.114
statue of man in -, XII.16
"The veil...", I.39
"We have made...", I.113
"When the word...", IX.48

Qutb
I.29
V.25
IX.128, 130
XI.216

Quwwat-e-Maknatis
IV.66

Rabia
V.187
X.68

Race
II.40

Racism
I.18

Radiance
II.112
IV.182
XI.41, 56
XII.13
- of face, XIII.233-4
- of soul, V.254-6

Radio
II.181, 260

Rag
II.53

Raga(s)
II.45, 53, 90, 98, 103, 110, 124
V.31
X.226

Ragini
II.53

Rahemat Khan
XII.129

Rahm
V.193

Rain
V.91

Rajas
II.242
IV.70
V.211
VIII.146
X.221
XI.22, 110
XIII.248

Raja Yoga
VII.209-10
XII.103
- best for Western life, XII.105

Rajputs
XIII.42

Rakshasa(s)
II.45
III.132
V.100
XII.41

Rama
II.188
VI.196
VII.63, 172
IX.144, 158-9, 269
X.188
XIII.28
Rama Muti
VII.103
Ramayana
VII.129
XIII.28
Rana
VII.63, 129
Raqs
I.43
II.46, 57, 61
IX.115
Rasa Shastra
- (book), III.115-96
X.214
Rasul
I.14, 29, 47
V.186
IX.128, 130-1, 133, 134, 136-7, 147
X.85-6
XI.160, 166
XII.133
Ray
VIII.154
Reaction
VI.98-102
VIII.292
XI.30
Real
IX.107
Reality
II.164
IV.270
XI.15-9, 151-2, 162, 227
illusion and -, XI.15-9
- above reason, XIII.251
search for -, XI.17
Realization
I.27, 44, 79, 81, 231
II.97, 109, 162, 169, 177
IV.156
V.17, 242
VI.121, 124, 139, 147, 204, 274
VII.197
VIII.162, 169
IX.13, 96, 106, 120, 142, 279
X.27-9, 49, 68, 136
XI.17, 223
XII.75
highest -, X.26
mystical -, IX.230
prayer of -, IX.38
- of God, XI.253
- of inner life, I.78-81
self--, V.250-1; VI.160-7, 207-16
spiritual -, I.148; IX.96; XI.243
Reason
I.96
II.240
III.79
IV.118, 139-40, 169
VII.84, 92
VIII.271, 278, 296
IX.53, 56-8, 144, 165-6, 175, 219, 230
XI.102
XII.43, 45
XIII.74, 251-2
earthly -, II.241
heavenly -, II.241
-ing, XI.108
- is earthborn, XIII.74-5
subtle -ing, IX.167
veils of -, X.23
Rebirth
I.81
Receptivity
II.150
Reciprocity
I.17
VI.237
IX.249
XI.131
law of -, I.17; III.233-42; IX.267; XI.179-82
Reconstruction

world -, X.248-51

Record
VI.233

Reed
IX.216-7, 242

Refinement
III.227
XI.243

Reflection
I.185
II.40, 168, 227, 248, 257
IV.199, 243, 245, 251, 257, 261-2, 281
V.92
IX.39, 229

Reform
VII.178

Reformation, the
IX.213, 251
XIII.91

Refuge
IX.85

Regularity
III.97
IV.19
XI.106

Reincarnation
I.130, 154
IV.269-270
V.121-30
VI.229-231
VIII.110, 163-72, 177
IX.157, 168
karma and -, VIII.163-72
- of mind, V.115

Rejection
I.31

Relations
I.214-5
our dealings with -, III.244-5

Relationship
III.201
VIII.216, 313
blood -, III.128
- with God, I.70; IX.109

Relativity
VIII.200
XIII.280

- of gain, III.258

Relaxation
III.19
IV.112, 162, 167
VIII.152
mystic -, IV.162-74

Relief
IX.46

Religion(s)
I.16, 17, 53, 150, 213, 216, 221
II. 149, 184
III.37, 126
IV.204
VI.13, 103-4
VII.21, 105, 168, 179
IX.11, 15-19, 21-9, 35, 102, 110, 118, 120, 147, 164, 173, 181, 236-7, 248-50, 256, 268-70, 274-5, 279
X.17, 255-7
XI.165, 173, 223, 236, 242, 255-6
XII.42, 56
ancient -s, IX.213
art and -, X.168-71
authority in -, IX.121
body and soul of -, IX.17
coming world -, IX.21-5
comparative -, XII.132
differences of -, VII.21; IX.117
degeneration of -, IX.241
democrary in -, IX.121
essence of -, XII.86
five aspects of -, IX.22-4, 275
form(s) of -, VII.26-7; IX.204
ideal of -, IX.22-3
intention of -, IX.196
lack of -, IX.36
law of -, IX.200
living -, IX.24
mission of -, IX.21
nature's -, VII.21-31
need of -, X.252-4
real -, XII.86
- and history, XII.135
- and life, VII.198

- and principles, XII.135
- is faith, VII.90
- of the day, IX.255
- of the heart, IX.19-20
-s, IX.247
source and goal of -, XI.256
spirit of -, VI.132
theme of -, IX.250
true -, I.145; III.139
work of -, IX.14

Religiosity
I.18, 102

Remedy
- for nerves, IV.37

Remembering
XI.49

Renaissance
X.175-6, 195

Renunciation
I.207-8
III.254-6
VI.89, 238-9
VII.122
VIII.74-9, 121
IX.133, 257
XI.181-2, 234, 247, 253
XII.78
forced -, III.254
law of -, III.254-62
learning of -, III.260-1
nature of -, III.261-2
necessity of -, III.257-8
- and loss, III.259-60

Repentance
V.197-9
VII.51
IX.43-4
XIII.292

Repetition(s)
I.152
II.159, 167, 172
IV.251
X.26
power of -, XI.91
- of a sound, XII.121
vain -, II.160

Repose
I.67-9
II.83, 95, 237
IV.99, 131, 194
X.47-50
XII.23
physical -, IV.99
- and action, XII.23
- of mind, IV.112

Representative
- of God, IX.141

Repulsion
XI.105
attraction and -, III.123
cause of -, III.124
law of -, XI.113
- and attraction, XII.39

Resignation
I.124
IV.161
VII.48, 51
VIII.68-73, 101, 137-8
IX.37, 104, 108-9, 133
XI.101, 162
XII.21
struggle and -, VIII.68-73
- vs. laziness, VIII.83

Resistance
true -, VII.47

Resonance
I.155
II.39, 56, 107, 121
IX.36

Respect
I.52, 204
III.55
VII.223-4
VIII.237-8
IX.34, 180, 261, 264, 266
XII.68
XIII.194-8
- and consideration, VIII.237-8
- first ideal, III.55, 72

Response
- in love, III.148

Responsibility
I.217
II.177, 221
IV.268
VI.268-271

VIII.36-7
IX.95, 193
XI.254
human -, IX.28

Responsiveness
IV.209
VII.150
IX.20, 125, 128, 268

Rest
IV.194
VII.124
XII.110

Restlessness
I.151
XI.239

Restrictions
IX.199

Resurrection
I.185, 205
V.219
VIII.180-3
IX.225
XI.210
XIII.95
mystical meaning of -, VIII.181-3
philosophy of -, V.219-21

Revelation
I.39, 56
II.191, 261
IV.214, 227
V.200
VI.108, 130-1, 150
VII.86
VIII.35, 314
IX.139, 265
X.51
dreams and -s, IV.210-4
faculty of -, XII.104
- to Muhammed, VIII.37

Revenge
III.235

Revolution
IX.126
Russian -, VII.121

Rewa
X.228

Rhythm(s)
I.42, 67, 147, 209-11
II.29, 35, 44-9, 50, 51, 52, 54, 74, 81, 89,93, 103, 121, 141, 143, 163, 217, 235, 242
III.21, 182
IV.15, 18-20, 60, 73-4, 162
VI.72-3, 75
VII.142
VIII.59, 146, 158
X.212, 222
XI.30-1, 44, 241
XII.112
XIII.15, 85, 141
destructive -, XI.239
disorder in -, III.182
kinds of -, VIII.146; XI.22-3
law of -, XI.44-8
musical -, XI.44
natural -, VI.42
obstruction of -, XI.46
rajas -, VIII.146
regular -, XI.106
- and impulse, VIII.146
- cause of formation, XI.45
- in infancy, XI.155
- of body, XI.47
- of breath, XI.31; XIII.141-2, 149-50
- of mind, XI.31, 47, 110
- of soul, XI.48
- of space, XI.34
- of thinking, VIII.40
right and wrong -, XI.47
satva -, VIII.146
tamas -, VIII.46
three kinds of -, IV.73
types of-, III.17; XIII.248

Right
X.52
- and wrong, I.17, 57; III.250; IV.109; V.216; VI.170, 235, 250; VIII. 249; XIII.279

Righteousness
I.49
IX.189-90, 208

Rind

VIII.16
X.85
XII.113
XIII.260
- vs. Salik, VIII.16
Risalat
I.14
IX.242
Rishi(s)
II.45
IX.158
Rituals
XI.145
Rivalry
IX.248
Roads
VI.202
Rocks
XI.63
Roman Catholic Church
IX.162
XI.236
Romans
X.205, 256
Rose
- and the unfoldment of the soul, VIII.295-7
Roza
IX.198
Ruba'iyat
II.232
Ruh
I.160
IV.197
V.26, 83
Ruh Allah
IX.147
Ruhi
V.29
Rules
I.82
Rumi
(see Jelal-ud-Din Rumi)
Russia
XII.155
XIII.17
Czar of -, XII.42
Rust
IV.264
XIII.232-3
- and mirror, IV.264
Rustam
XII.71

Sabtal
XII.112
Sabz
V.162
Sabzpari
V.162-3
Sacrament
IX.187, 218
philosophy of the -, IX.187-8
Sacred
I.56
- scriptures, X.120
Sacredness
IX.207, 241
Sacrifice
I.219
IV.123
V.194
VI.155
VIII.75, 295, 322
IX.133, 171-2, 182
X.101
XI.181, 251, 253, 255, 259
Sadhana
VI.195
XII.106
Sadhu
XII.106
Sa'di, Muslih-ud-Din
I.16
II.262
III.121, 149, 215
IV.175, 194, 204, 228
V.11, 22, 204, 240
VI.34, 59, 66, 115, 268
VII.18, 66, 68, 86, 148, 179
VIII.14, 114, 139, 200, 202, 294
IX.41-2, 106
X.130, 141-6

XI.123, 134
XII.58, 144
XIII.40, 59
"Every being...", VIII.294
"Every leaf...", VII.179
"Every soul...", I.16, 189; VIII.139
"He who depends...", IX.106
"Let me confess...", VIII.202
"Lord, I have...", IX.44
"Once I had...", VIII.114
"The Creator...", IX.93

Sadik
VIII.14

Sadness
I.150
XI.244, 247-8, 253

Sadrat al Manteha
V.32

Saf
I.161
VI.240
VIII.23
IX.189, 200, 253

Safa
V.16
VIII.15
XII.106
XIII.51-2

Safety
IX.85

Sage
VIII.267
X.30-1
XI.242
XII.106, 113, 115
Chinese -, XIII.104
life of - in East, XII.106-17
master, - and prophet, IX.132-5
presence of -, XII.117
renunciation of -s, III.262
- in Bengal, IV.117
-s of India, IV.284

Sahabis
V.21

Saheba-e-Safa
V.21

Sahib-e Dil
V.28, 73
VI.221
XI.114

Saint
I.101, 220
IV.163
VII.30
IX.38, 129, 132-4
XI.180
XII.106, 109
path of -, XIII.275
-ly, IX.108, 143
-ly temperament, VI.222
-s, I.157; IX.145
song to soul of -, I.27-8
spirit of -, IX.133

Saki
II.74
VIII.122, 228
X.125
Bowl of -, XIII.110

Sala'm
V.209

Salat
IX.197, 272

Salik
VIII.16
IX.252
X.85
XII.113-6, 145
- vs. Rind, VIII.16

Salim
XIII.194

Salima
V.25
XI.203

Salt
IX.219-20

Saluk
VIII.264
XIII.167-204

Salvation
II.139
VIII.172
IX.17, 181

Sama
(see also Suma)
XIII.31

Samadhi
I.142
II.77, 141
IV.202
V.86, 198
X.139
XIII.31
Samat
V.26
Sami
VIII.197
XII.61
- and Basir, XII.61
Samwadi
II.54
Sand
IV.163
Sandow
VII.102
San Francisco
XII.152
Sangam
V.134
VII.54
VIII.278
XIII.162
Sangita
II.92
Sankha
IX.207
Sankrian
II.45
Sannyasa-shrama
VII.210
XII.110, 112
Sannyasi
XII.116
Sansara
VIII.247
Sanskrit
II.96, 158, 179
X.94, 212-4, 216-7, 232-4
Sant
XII.106-8
Sanyasi
V.121
Sarasvati
II.75
IX.207
X.185
XIII.123
Sarmad
I.83
V.198
Satan
III.185
V.105
VI.94
VII.14
VIII.97, 186
IX.178
X.267-9
XIII.183
- (ego), XII.90
Sati
II.232
III.171
X.40
Satisfaction
I.144
V.94
VI.191
IX.85
XI.257
Saturday
XIII.43
Satva (Sattwa)
II.242
IV.70, 163
V.211
VIII.146
IX.201
XI.22, 110
XIII.248
-, rajas, tamas, IV.70; V.211
Saum
- and Salat, IX.272
Saut
V.32
Saut-e Sarmad
I.180
II.62, 67, 203
Saviour
IX.185
Saving
IV.235

XII.59

Sayings:

"All's well that ends well", IX.108

"Man proposes, God disposes", IX.108

Sayn Aliyas

VII.249

Scandanavia

-n myth, XIII.110-1

Scepticism

IX.233

School

esoteric -s, IX.252

Sufi -s, IX.88

Science

II.90, 96, 121, 174, 185

IV.266

VI.129

X.259

XI.73-4, 119, 146

XII.82, 12

age of -, IX.63

- and psychology, XI.73-4

- of human nature, XI.123

Scientist

- and word "within", IV.189

mystic and -, XII.82

Scriabin

II.138

X.229

Scripture(s)

I.16

VII.178

IX.146, 149-151, 158, 234, 236, 265, 272, 274, 279

XI.171

Jewish -, IX.146

original Buddhist -, IX.167

purpose of -, IX.12

Zoroastrian -, IX.177

Sculpture

X.120, 186-95

Sea

VI.40

VIII.367-8, 318

waves of -, XI.68

Seal(s)

IX.27, 151

Séance

XIII.28

Searching

IX.75

Seasickness

remedy for -, IX.53-4

Seclusion

XIII.20, 22-4

Secrecy

I.50-1

Secret

IX.249

keeping a -, XIII.260-1

- of God, IX.151

- of success, IX.253

- of the messenger, IX.238

- of the soul, XI.240

- of things, XI.15-6

to keep a -, VIII.40

Sectarianism

IX.261

Seed

IV.115

IX.118

man, - of God, V.131-7; VIII.123-7

- of man, III.127

-s of the rose, VIII.297

Seeing

I.79

VIII.39-44

IX.137

XI.56

XII.21

natural -, VIII.302

- and overlooking, VIII.241-2

- behind things, VIII.321

Seeking

VI.257

VIII.126

- for God, IX.85

Seen

- and unseen, V.213-4

Seer

I.85-6

IV.259

VI.154

VIII.40-1, 196, 302-3
IX.110, 213, 228
XI.74
XII.20, 74
glance of -, XIII.54-5
-s, IX.145

Self
I.24
VI.12
VIII.18-9, 188
IX.114, 133, 174, 242
XI.150-1, 197-8, 203, 242, 244, 247
breath, vehicle of -, XIII.142-3
consciousness of -, IX.115
development of -, XI.140
external -, VIII.119
false -, XI.250
killing the -, XII.93
knowledge of -,I.200-6; IX.110
loss of -, XI.163
love of -, VIII.114
natural and spiritual -, IX.171
negation of -, IX.90
real -, I.98; VII.189; VIII.187
real, natural -, XII.102
--analysis, XI.151
- and merit of God, IX.102-4
--healing, IV.89
--obsession, XI.165
- of God, IX.51, 101-3
--pride, XII.41
--sufficiency, VII.111
studying your-, VII.162
true -, VIII.149; XI.250

Self-assertion
VII.191

Self-confidence
IV.224
VII.90
XII.44
XIII.245

Self-consciousness
I.185
XIII.177-8, 179

Self-control
III.199-200, 220
IV.71
VI.102, 221
IX.172
XIII.259

Self-denial
I.19, 52, 204-5, 207, 224
IV.169
VI.100, 155, 172
IX.91, 174, 177, 216, 224, 267
XI.234, 241
XIII.94, 184

Self-discipline
I.207, 235
VI.198
VIII.45-8

Self-effacement
I.204-5
VIII.18
IX.224

Self-interest
IX.262

Selfish
VIII.113, 122, 190, 216, 277
XI.131-2
foolish - and wise -, VII.122

Selfishness
I.145
VII.113, 164-6
IX.93, 197-8, 246, 249
XI.128
XIII.176

Self-knowledge
I.20-1, 202, 235
V.16-7
XI.196-200

Selfless
VIII.130-1, 134, 189

Selflessness
I.145, 174
VIII.230-1
IX.113
XIII.203-4

Self-pity
III.198
VI.50-158
VIII.113-4
XI.235, 258

Self-realization
I.88, 145-6, 162

V.250-1
VI.188, 207
IX.81, 97, 253-4, 266
X.87, 97-8
XI.199, 253
XII.19
inner life and -, VI.160-7
stages on the path of -, VI.207-215
the inner life and -, VI.160-7

Self-respect
III.221
IV.52
XIII.181
inspiring - in infant, III.41

Self-righteousness
I.23

Self-sacrifice
I.29

Seman
III.235

Sensation
I.209, 211
IV.114, 131
VIII.152

Sense
inner -, XI.29-30, 231
principal -, XIII.67

Senses
I.80, 148, 152
II.130, 191, 229, 231
IV.57
V.26, 231
XI.29-30, 36, 231
XII.83
five -, XI.42
nature of - and their organs, V.231-2
organs of -, XI.20

Sensitiveness
I.152, 181
VI.84
IX.20, 222, 278
XIII.184

Sensitivity
I.100

Sentiment
VIII.271
X.43-4
XIII.219

Sentimentality
IV.142

Separatiom
V.161
IX.142

Sermon
- on the Mount, VI.88

Serpent
I.100
IV.103
VI.211
- quality, I.100

Servant
our dealings with -s, III.245-6
- aspect in man, VII.159
- of mankind, I.103-4

Server
I.103, 214
XI.237, 241, 246

Service
I.52, 100, 214, 240
IX.20, 177, 266, 270
XI.235, 246
- to humanity, I.103-4, X.93

Sex
(see also Rasa Shastra)
III.119-191 passim
V.93
positive and negative aspects of -, III.119-20
purpose of -, III.127
opposite -, III.143

Shadow
XI.125, 237
psychology of -, XIII.33-4
- of sudra, XIII.33-4
-s, IV.269

Shah Alam
VIII.197

Shah Jehan
X.215

Shah Kamush
VIII.209

Shah-nameh
V.137
VI.129

Shah of Persia
X.129
Shaikh
I.42
V.186
Shakespeare
X.218, 233
XII.75
Shakti
VII.12
Shame
IX.24
XI.232
XIII.289-92
Shams-e Tabrez
II.38
III.173
IV.90, 284
VIII.14
X.137-8, 216
XII.74
- and Shah, IV.90
"When the sun...", I.113
Shankani
III.136
Shankaracharya
I.130
VIII.208
IX.209
Shaqqu's-Sadr
V.230
IX.228-30
XIII.120-1
Sharda
XII.136
Shariat
VII.33-4
IX.199
XII.69
Sharif
II.67
Sharif-ud-Din
V.22
Sharing
IX.246
XIII.198
Sheep
II.26
Shekinah
I.53
Sherab-i Kouthar
V.181
Shighravaki
V.112
X.217
Shihab-ud-Din Sohrawardi
V.22
Shirin and Farhad
V.150-4
VI.116
Shirvan Bhagat
V.147
Shiva
(see also Mahadeva)
II. 62, 75, 98, 103
IV.193
V.196
VIII.249-50
IX.108, 147, 206, 218
X.188, 222
XI.49, 117, 167
XII.105
XIII.54, 73, 273, 286-7
- Bhaktis, XIII.295
- eating fish, XIII.213
- followers, XIII.114-5
-ji, VI.35
Shortcomings
rejecting impressions of -, XIII.235-6
Shrine
-of God, IX.193, 229
Shuhud
V.88, 143, 230
Shukhi
III.134
Shushumna
XIII.95
Siam
X.203
Sickness
I.159
Siddhi
V.73
VI.195
Siddiq

V.21
IX.199

Sifat
I.163
II.130
V.14
IX.102, 196

Sifat Allah
V.36
IX.102

Sight
II.128, 177
IX.103
XI.56

Silence
II.161, 184, 242
III.23, 203
IV.204-9, 214, 217
VII.39, 43
VIII.206-10
IX.135
X.47
XI.63, 212
natural inclination is -, VII.39
pleasure in -, VII.41
power of -, VIII.206-10

Silver Age
I.220-1
X.223

Simplicity
II.126
VII.239
VIII.287
XI.117,
- and complexity, VII.239-44

Sin
I.19, 59
VII.61
VIII.99, 215, 231, 233
IX.39, 115, 178, 181
XI.245-6
XII.30
XIII.271-2
forgiveness of -s, IX.181-2
- and virtue, I.17; VII,132
word -, XIII.271-3

Sinai, Mount
IX.258

Sincerity
I.26
III.110
IV.184
VI.127
VIII.188
IX.102, 121
X.74
XII.99
XIII.169
sense of beauty and -, XIII.169-71

Singer
II.56

Singh, Maharaja Ronjit
II.224

Singing
IX.38

Sirajs
IX.272

Sita
II.188
IX.158

Sitar
II.56

Sitara
V.25

Sleep
I.142, 196
IV.131, 195, 213
V.85
VII.130
VIII.193, 304, 308, 310-11, 317-8
IX.119
XII.51, 64
mystery of -, IV.195-203; VIII.193-5
- of confusion, I.51-2
waking from -, I.190; VIII.117, 306-7

Slipping
XI.160

Smile
III.205
VI.120
XI.234, 244
learning to -, III.206

Smoking
XIII.217
Snake
- charmers, II.54, 110; IV.244
Soberness
I.184
IV.36
VI.141, 143
IX.98, 110, 112
X.125-6
Sobriety
I.17, 184
XIII.217-8
Sociability
III.110, 112
Social life
IX.32
Socrates
VIII.14
Sohrwardi
- school, VIII.18
Soil
IX.254
Solar-plexus
I.155
Solitude
VIII.35
Solomon
I.33, 208, 230
V.200
VII.170, 172
IX.142, 247
X.148
XI.167
XII.132-3
"...nothing new...", VII.39
story of -, I.208
'ution
IX.249
-omeone
IX.83
Son
IX.216
only-begotten -, IX.141
- of God, V.115; IX.120, 181
Song Celestial, the
IX.161
Sophia
II.165
VI.240
IX.252
Sorbonne
XII.155
Sorrow(s)
VI.123
IX.216, 234
XI.253
XIII.288-89
Soul(s)
I.21, 44, 51, 81, 114-5, 124, 127-9, 160, 165-85, 206
II.55, 58, 79, 96, 100, 128, 187, 215, 223, 246, 259
IV.71
V.92, 133, 137, 252
VI.11, 19, 20, 27, 191
VIII.175, 178, 193-4, 281, 292
IX.18, 26, 52, 75, 83, 88, 93, 96, 97, 100, 102, 111, 114, 116, 117, 120-122, 167, 182, 217, 220-1, 228, 237-8, 255, 258, 266
X.40-2, 127
XI.21, 41, 68-9, 104, 116, 134, 135, 140, 146, 153, 201, 228-9, 231-6, 238-9, 242, 245-6, 248, 255-9
XII.16
XIII.51
angelic quality of -, VIII.155, 266
awakening of -, VII.195-7; VIII.302-22
birthright of -, IX.174
body and -, V.42
child - and old -, III.198
condition of -, XI.153
connection of - with mind and body, V.253-4
consciousness and -, V.236
dance of the -, VII.242; VIII.328-32
departed -, I.169-71
desire of -, I.122, 172; VIII.76, 298-301; XI.239
destiny of -, V.247-56

divine origin of -, VIII.177
effect of prayer on -, IX.37
emotions of -, V.243
error of -, I.185
evolution of -, IX.218
experiences of -, V.240-6
fine -, I.99
five bodies of -, IX.219-20
food for every -, IX.137
freedom of the -, VII.180-97
godly -, IX.112-3
greatest -s, VIII.284
heart and -, V.28
human -, XI.258
illuminated -s, V.109; VI.235; VII.226; IX.137, 174; XI.248, 257
inherent attribute in -, IX.202
inheritance of -, IV.278
innate yearning of -, IX.201
journey of -, I.129, 184; V.92, 113; VIII.155-62
kinds of -s, I.124-5
kingdom of -, IX.223
light and -, V.251
light of -, XI.254
living -, IX.24, X.119-20
longing of -, IX.91-2
lost -, IX.25
magnetism of -, XI.116
manifestation of -, VIII.179-80
maturity of -, VIII.323-7; IX.28, 85
mind and -, V.237, 242, 253
motive of -, IX.192
nature of -, V.245; VII.188; IX.11
original -, IX.221
Phenomenon of the -, The (book), V.79-137
philosophy of -, V.83-6
privilege of every -, XI.172
prophetic -, IX.140, 144-51; XI.254
purpose of -, VIII.38
radiance of -, V.254-6
recognition of -, V.252
reincarnation of -, VIII.167-70
rhythm of -, XI.48
saintly -, XI.181
secret of -, XI.240
seeking -, XI.148
- after death, V.43, 106
- as light of God, XIII.223
- as ray of sun, XI.68
- choosing parents, V.92
- in itself alone, V.236-7
- like caterpillar, IV.266
-mate, IX.158-9
- of the age, IX.30
-, origin and unfoldment, VIII.288-93
--power, V.256
-, satisfaction of every, IX.20
-'s desire, VIII.298-301
-'s experience, V.105-11
-'s return to God, V.105
-, *Whence and Whither?, The* (book), I.107-85
- with mind, V.237-8
- with mind and body, V.238
spiritual -s, I.102-6; IX.95; XI.156
sustenance of -, IX.189
twin -s, VIII.93; XI.129-33
two vehicles of -, VIII.290
unfoldment of -, VIII.288-97; XI.117
winter of -, VIII.176

Sound
I.155
II.14, 62, 79, 85, 92, 106, 111, 121, 127, 133, 157, 162, 185, 237
III.24
XI.25, 212
abstract -, II.62-7
colour and -, XIII.144-5
effect of - on physical body, II.110
healing with -, II.14
inner -, II.62, 203
manifestation of - on physical plane, II.1069
mystery of - and colour, II.121-6

Mysticism of -, The (book), II.9-67
mystic use of -, XII.119-20
physical effect of -, II.110
repetition of -, II.112
- of air, II.15
- of earth, II.15
- of ether, II.16
- of fire, II.15
- of water, II.15
spiritual significance of - and colour, II.127-34

Source
I.25, 165
IV.87, 115
IX.75

South Pole
IX.219

Sovereign
I.209
IX.202

Sovereignty
IX.223

Sowing
- seed, IX.37

Space
IV.87
VI.228
IX.191
XI.34, 54, 63-4, 210-12, 221, 241, 249

Spark
divine -, I.230; IX.20, 118, 139

Speaker
XI.120

Speaking
I.148
II.29
IV.102
IX.178

Speed
I.147

Speech
II.29, 185, 204

Sphere
I.141, 146
VI.226
VII.241
XI.153, 234
music of the -s, II.78-84

Sphinx
VII.106

Spine
XIII.140

Spirit
I.15, 20, 52, 78, 88, 117, 124-6, 195-6, 225
II.17, 37, 73, 85, 100, 108, 118, 148, 215, 251, 261
III.101, 110
IV.39, 68-9, 99, 108, 114, 187
VI.41, 48, 196-7
VII.149, 151, 229-30, 232, 239-40
VIII.153-4, 178-80, 288-9, 317
IX.81, 103, 139, 171, 217-8, 233, 238, 240
X.48, 103
XI.22, 57-62, 63-9, 73, 91, 203, 206, 208, 228-9, 241, 243-4, 249, 251
XII.17
condition of one's -, XI.208
conservative -, VIII.232-3
divine -, I.111, 113, 115, 135, 185; IX.20, 96, 229, 247
four explanations of -, X.36-43
God's own -, IX.184
guiding -, IX.267
language of -, I.183
living -, IX.237
nature of -, XI.62
poor in -, V.194
poorness of -, VII.66-7
qualities of -, IX.90
saintly -, XI.163
secret of -, X.36-42
- and matter, V.27; XI.57-69
- communication, IV.249; V.70
--conscious, IX.238
--consciousness, XI.65
- of Christ, IX.183-7
- of God, IX.179, 188, 225; XIII.191-2
- of prophecy, I.34-8
- of Sufism, IX.256-8

-s and spiritism, VII.149-52
-s of animals, V.71
- within, XIII.29
- within and without, XI.53-6
tuning of -, XI.205-9

Spirit of Guidance
I.15, 31
VI.149
VII.226
IX.139-43, 149, 166, 226, 240, 242
X.218
XIII.125

Spirit of Prophecy
I.34

Spirits
II.52
V.63
IX.205
- and illness, IV.24
- and spiritism, VII.149-52

Spiritual
VIII.211, 220, 222-3, 271-2, 278-80, 286-7, 295
XI.235
condition of - person, XI.156
- atmosphere, VIII.283
- attainment, VIII.270, 282, 290
- culture, XI.62
- development, XI.155
- exercises, VIII.159
- hierarchy, IX.125-31
- is natural, VIII.280-1
- liberation, VIII.166
- man, XI.15
- means natural, IV.99
- person, I.224; VI.19; VIII.54-5
- personality, VIII.284
- realization, VIII.212
- unfoldment, VIII.29

Spiritualiam
V.67-71

Spirituality
I.117, 176-7
III.236
IV.39, 42,68, 113, 225
V.27
VI.17, 149, 95, 243
VIII.55, 154, 183, 279, 288, 306
IX.102, 162, 238, 253
X.122
XI.236, 243
XIII.183, 266-7
losing -, IX.38

Spiritual Path
II.177
VI.41
IX.96, 101-2, 148, 255
XI.69, 121
XII.88
progress on -, II.120

Sports
II.44

Stages
III.30
X.82, 88-9
- of action, IX.245

Standard(s)
IX.97
XIII.226-7

Star
IV.76
IX.268
XIII.98

State
duty to -, I.215

Statue
- of Liberty, IX.167

Steadfastness
I.90

Stillness
III.112
IV.99, 147
VII.129

Stone
- of Jesus's tomb, VIII.182
philosopher's -, IX.118
- quality, XI.156

Stories:
- about a fish, XI.18
- (fable) of camel and donkey, III.208
- in India, XI.130

- of a Brahmin, XI.125
- of adept in ship, IV.283
- of a juggler, XI.222
- of a king, XI.208
- of Alif, I.40-1
- of a Maharaja, XI.138
- of a mystic, XI.215-6
- of an opium-eater, XI.124
- of a Persian king, XI.115
- of Arab rider, IV.242
- of Arab running to mosque, IX.64
- of a robber, XI.175-6
- of artist in studio (Una), IV.287
- of Aurangzeb, VI.160
- of Ayaz, III.216-7; XI.82, 208
- of Bayazid, IV.54
- of Brahmin and idol, IX.67
- of boy going to Baghdad, VII.117
- of businessman who failed, IV.255
- of dervish and soldier, XII.89-90
- of dog and loaf, VIII.76-7
- of donkey and camel, III.65
- of Eastern king, III.160
- of elephants in forest, IX.184
- of enthusiastic servant, III.208
- of farmer making lantern, IX.183
- of farmer's boy and Moses, VII.27-8
- of girl and Muslim, IX.64
- of girl and theatrical song, IV.253
- of good husbandman, III.175
- of great mystic in mosque, IV.139
- of Hafiz Shirazi, IV.93
- of Haris Chandra, III.223; VI.246
- of holy mand who said he was a thief, IV.187
- of housemaid of Moghul king, VII.156-7
- of hunter killing bird, III.170
- of Indian prostitute, III.190
- of jinn who wanted to amuse, I.233
- of king's parrot, VII.185-6
- of king's servant, VIII.227-8
- of king who prays, IX.47
- of Lahu and Kusha, VII.63, 129
- of Lot's wife, IX.218-21
- of magician, IV.230
- of Maharaja Rajit Singh, VI.247-8
- of Maharana of Udaipur, IX.34
- of maid and angry man, IX.64
- of Majnun and Leila, IX.23
- of man avoiding "church", IX.73
- of man called to Sinai, I.34-8
- of man in dark room, IX.75
- of man under cherry tree, VIII.83
- of man who did bad things, IV.234
- of Mira Bai, III.167-9
- of Moses, VI.212
- of Moses and Khizr, IX.105
- of Moses and peasant, IX.71-2
- of Moslem and Brahmin, IV.174
- of Muhammad, VI.265; VIII.63, 70, 164
- of Muhammad and dates, IV.91
- of Muhammad on battlefield, IV.182-3
- of Muhammad's enemy, III.130
- of mureed, VIII.71
- of mureed who wanted to see heaven, VII.127-8
- of "My mother is best", IX.271

- of Nawab of Rampur, III.24-5
- of peasants travelling, IV.179
- of Persian king and dervish, VII.172
- of prayer of peasant, IX.51-2
- of preacher and peasant, VII.96
- of prince sent away, IV.185
- of Prime Minister of Hyderabad, VI.265-6
- of Prophet's enemy, VII.93
- of Puran Bhagat, VII.74
- of rich man in park, IV.121
- of Rustam and Kusham, XII.71-2
- of Sa'di, IX.41-2
- of sage in India, IV.109
- of schoolboy who was jinn, VII.160
- of Shaikh Khamush, IV.217
- of Shams, IV.90
- of Shankaracharya and disciple, IV.279
- of Shirin and Farhad, IV.
- of Shivaji, XI.173
- of son of famous teacher, XII.97
- of Sufi, VIII.244
- of Sufi in caravan, VII.93-4
- of telegraph cleark, IV.172
- of the Rajput Raja, VI.248-9
- of the three horsemen, XI.149
- of tree of fulfillment of desire, VII.135; VIII.115
- of Turkish father and son, III.155
- of two madzubs, VII.114
- of two Sufis, VIII.244
- of young girl speaking Persian, IV.280
- of Zeb-un-Nissa, III.140
-: parable of dog, VII.50

Strength
I.142, 173
II.227
IX.98
XI.250

Strife
IX.93

Struggle
VI.90
VIII.68, 107
IX.144, 159
XI.137, 159
XII.27
man's -, IX.93
- and resignation, VIII.68-73
- for existence, I.146
- of life, VI.87-97

Student
X.104

Study
X.89
XII.102
inner -, X.87-90
- of life, VI.104; X.87, 89

Stupidity
IX.111

Subconscious
II.226
XI.49

Sublimity
- of nature,IX.48

Substance
XI.22, 60-1, 63

Subtle
- and gross, IV.113-8

Subtlety
III.203-4
IV.113
XI.243
- in nature, X.187

Success
I.219
IV.201
VI.201
VII.52
XI.80, 236, 240
secret of -,IX.253
- and failure, IV.104, 199

Sudras
V.125
IX.156

Suffering(s)

VII.166-7
IX.95, 217, 223-4
X.211
XI.159
XIII.220

Sufi
(see also following entries through Sufism))
I.45-60
VII.43, 122
VIII.13-6,109,170, 178, 181, 226, 264, 283, 287
XI.139, 159, 162-3, 175, 188
XII.71, 75
aim of -, VIII.24-
history of -, VIII.12-17
idea of -, VIII.225
ideal of -, IX.264-6
meaning of -, XII.29
sign of -, VIII.243
- and balance, VIII.222
- and love, VII.18
- esoteric studies, IV.151
- from Persia, VIII.324
- ideal, XII.29-32
- ideal of God, VII.32
- message, V.9-36, IX.247-51
- method, IV.254, 256
- *Mysticism* (book), X.9ff
- path, VIII.112
- poet, XI.139
- poetic imagery, X.123-5
- *Poetry* (book), X.115ff
- poets, XII.113
- psychology, XII.38-41
- Publishing Society, XII.155
- sages, XII.113-4
-'s aim in life, IX.259-63
-'s conception of God, IX.113-5
-'s journey, IX.83
-'s way, XII.88
- symbol, IX.87, 268-70
- *Teachings* (book), VIII
- thoughts, I.13-22; IX.267
- training, V.24
- view of God as beloved, VIII.138, 200
what is a -?, VIII.26-7

Sufi Message
VIII.20
IX.16, 20, 148, 248, 262, 269
XIII.271-3

Sufi Movement
I.50
VII.179
IX.20, 148, 249, 252, 255, 262-3, 267-73
X.131, 257-8, 261, 265-6, 269-70
XII.50
purpose of -, IX.270-3
symbol of -, IX.268-70
three objects of the -, IX.267-8
purpose of the -, IX.270-3
symbol of the -, IX.268-70

Sufi Order
V.21-3
X.75, 79, 81
objects of -, XII.153
- in America, XII.153
symbol of -, XIII.97-9

Sufis
I.45-60, 143
II.165, 180, 218
V.16, 21
VI.30, 52, 58, 91, 272
IX.162, 172, 188-9, 199-200, 218, 221, 229, 252-3, 256-7, 266
X.48-50, 75-7, 85, 87, 88, 100, 106, 122-3, 125, 130, 111, 187, 197, 216-8
XI.50, 62, 140
XIII.19, 21, 53
Chistia Order of -, II.60, 77
history of -, VIII.13-7
Mevlevi Order of -, II.60
music among -, V.31-2
Rafai School of -, II.108
- , masters of breathing, IV.194-5
-'s aim, VIII.24-7
-'s aim in life, V.31-2
-'s conception, IX.276
-'s conception of God, IX.113-

-'s conception of God, IX.113-5
-'s ideal, II.31; IX.264-5
-'s moral, IX.265
-'s path, devotion, XIII.119
-'s schools, IX.88
-'s tombs, V.22
suma, music of -, I.41-4
work of -, XIII.267

Sufism
I.45, 53, 72, 161
V.16, 21-3, 27, 59, 191-2
VI.198
VII.145, 179
VIII.13, 18-23, 163
IX.20, 24-5, 112, 113, 115, 148, 171, 188, 200, 252-6, 264-5
X.49
XI.161, 232
XII.20-2, 30, 146
aspects of -, I.23-44
first moral of -, IX.20
history of -, VIII.13-23
principal mission of -, IX.254
principal teaching of -, XIII.98
secret of -, IX.167
schools of -, XII.149
spirit of -, IX.256-8
- , essence of all religions, V.222
- is wisdom, XIII.278

Sufragettes
XII.154

Suggestion(s)
IV.92
V.72
XI.75-89, 96, 127
XII.38
first -, XI.78
healing by -, IV.84-5
- by movement, XI.92-5
- by word and voice, XI.89-91
- in practice, XI.96-8
- in the name, XI.87
- through impression and belief, XI.80-4
- through various forms of impression, XI.85-8

Suicide
IV.24
VII.193
VIII.102-3

Suluk
(see also Saluk)
V.183
VII.255

Suma
I.41-2
II.57, 60, 94
V.32
IX.115
XII.146
-, music of Sufis, I.41-4

Sun
I.113
II.38
IV.28, 257
VI.227
VIII.153-4, 158, 306
IX.20, 119, 125, 176, 183, 214-5, 216, 258
X.41
XI.39, 42, 228, 234, 246-7, 256
XII.13
eternal -, IX.176
- as intelligence, VIII.296
- currents, IV.28
- of God, IX.120
-shine, XI.234
- worship, VII.23; IX.120, 155, 176, 215
symbolism of -, IX.214-5; XIII.92-3
symbol of -, IX.214-5

Sundar Das
poem on Guru, IX.156

Sunday
XIII.42

Superstition(s)
IV.260
VII.59
XII.38
XIII.11-2
-, customs and beliefs, XIII.11-

46
- of days in East, XIII.42-3
Sura
I.115, 179
II.92
Surdas
V.167
Surgery
IV.18, 32
Surrender
IX.202, 216
XI.162
Sushupti
IV.201
Suspicion
XI.124
Sustainer
I.216
IX.93
Svar-loka
I.136
Swaga
XII.106
Swansong
XIII.40-1
Swapna
IV.198
Sword
IX.163
Symbol
IX.214
- of cross, VIII.184-90; IX.190-1, 223-5; XIII.93-5
- of dove, IX.225-6; XIII.96-7
- of dragon, XIII.106-7
- of Sufi Movement, IX.268
- of Sufi Order, XIII.97-9
- of sun, IX.214; XIII.92-3
Symbolism
III.23, 138
IX.87, 213-30, 268
rebellion against -, XIII.92
- in child's action, III.23
- in religion, X.185, 189, 218-9; XIII.91-2
- of lines, XIII.100-1
- of triangle, XIII.101-2
Symbology
X.188-8
XIII.89-131
- of dot and circle, XIII.99-100
- of mushroom, XIII.102-3
- of religious ideas, IX.213-30; XIII.120-131
Sympathy
I.26, 31, 116
IV.124
VI.47
VII.16, 134, 168
VIII.271-2, 278, 293, 314
IX.20, 57, 100, 228, 261
XI.11-14, 55, 112, 140, 232
XII.99
XIII.269-71
development of -, VIII.282-3
path of -, VIII.284
- of mature soul, VIII.325
Symphony
VI.34
VIII.164
XI.254
Synthesis
XI.74

Taba'in
V.21
Taba'-i-taba'in
V.21
Tabla
I.43
II.56
Tact
XI.109
Tagore, Abanindranath
X.182
Tagore, Rabindranath
II.105
IV.278
VIII.137, 295
X.151
Tahajud
XII.140
Taj Mahal

IV.156
X.204-5, 215
Tala
II.45
X.224-5, 228
Talib
II.36
V.221
Talkativeness
IX.169
Tamas (Tammas)
II.242
III.207
IV.70, 163
V.162, 211
VIII.146
IX.201
XI.22, 110
XIII.248
Tambura
II.101
Tandeva Nrutya
II.45
Taneiev
II.138
Tansen
II.54, 116, 137
IV.72
X.228
XII.137
Tanzi(h)
I.112
V.25
- and Tashbi, I.112
Taqwa Taharat
XIII.207-239
Tarab
V.31
Taran
V.46
VII.183-4
IX.222
XIII.120
Tariqat
VII.34
IX.199-200
XII.69-70
Tark
I.56
Tasawwuf
XIII.241-296
Tasbih
V.25
Tashbi
I.112
Tat Tvam Asi
XIII.52-4
Taviz (charm)
IV.80
Tawajoh
IV.93, 278
X.76, 86
XII.103
Tawakul
VII.250
IX.106
XIII.264-5
Tawazeh
XIII.193, 198-9
Teacher
(see also Murshid)
I.14, 38
IV. 111, 142, 203
VI.68, 164
VII.113
VIII.105
IX.51, 155, 242, 268
X.16, 63, 65, 73, 88, 95-6, 102, 105-6, 109
XI.121, 140, 148
XII.103
inheritance from -, IV.278
lives of the -s, VIII.184; IX.127-8
loyalty to -, VII.22
name of the -, VII.225
spiritual -, I.15; VI.168
-s, I.32; XI.223
Sufi -, XI.140
world -, I.45-6
Teaching
inner -s, IX.199
- of the prophets, XI.258
openess to -, I.49-50
Sufi -s (book), VIII
-s from the past, IX.69-70

-s of the prophets, IX.180
Tears
IX.258
Telepathy
IV.264
V.241
the mystery of -, XII.60-7
Temperaments
I.222
XI.216
XII.106
Temple
V.231
Buddhist -, IX.167
foundation of world's new -, IX.245
- of Peace, IX.230
Temptation
XIII.252-3
Ten Commandments
IX.173
Tendency
persuasive -, III.219
prophetic -, VIII.32-8
Tenderness
III.159
IV.51
Tennyson
XII.161
Terms
some esoteric -, I.38-9
Test
I.220
IX.182
X.64101
man's -, I.220
Testing
X.109
Thankfulness
III.216
IV.51
V.11
IX.34, 38, 41
Thanksgiving
XI.251
Theft
intellectual -, X.104
Theme
- of religion, IX.250
Things
VI.236
XI.15, 39
distribution of -, XI.194
interest in all -, XIII.80-1
Thinker
XI.111
ascetic -, XI.194
Thinking
III.241
IV.136, 253
IX.178
XI.49, 74
- and imagination, IV.158.
Thorns
crown of -, IX.222
Thought(s)
I.26, 39
II.18, 204, 213, 222, 226, 238, 242, 251
IV.26, 148, 168, 250-2, 256, 273
V.44, 197
VI.219
VII.89, 133, 135-6
IX.149, 162
XI.54, 230
XII.83
XIII.69, 262-4
collective -, II.202
consciousness of -, IV.122
evil -, IX.229
evidence of -, XIII.69-70
five aspects of -, IV.148ff
life of -, II.220-5
power of -, IV.148-51; VII.132-3
Sufi -s, I.13-22; IX.267
- and imagination, II.226-30
-fulness, XI.103
- of God, Sufi, IX.115
- reading, XIII.158-9
Thousand and One Nights
VI.69
IX.183
XII.118, 123
Thread

- of the Parsis, IX.177
Throne
- of God, IX.234
Thursday
XIII.43
Tibet
X.193, 203
art of -, X.180-1
Time
I.114, 146-7
II.41, 73, 124, 177, 181
V.88, 149
IX.56, 162
XI.211-12, 241, 249
XIII.45
appointed -, X.50
influence of -, XIII.45-6
- and space, V.88
Timurlenk
VI.220
Tiredness
IV.61-2
VII.42
Tistra
II.45
Titanic
II.213
Toasts
XIII.35-9
Today
Yesterday, - and Tomorrow (book), X.155ff
Tolerance
I.53-4, 230-1
IV.151
VII.27
VIII.109, 127, 147
IX.18, 20, 37, 55, 161, 254, 277-8
XI.237
XIII.253-4, 292-4
Tone
II.51, 81, 121
IV.15, 17
XI.89, 241
Tongues
- of flame, I.118; IX.227-8; XIII.125
Touch
healing by -, IV.83
Toys
III.17, 44-5
Tragedy
II.218
VII.155, 191-2
IX.106
X.232
greatest -, IX.36
- of life, I.22; VII.180; IX.20, 115; XII.79-81
Training
III.81
V.24
mental -, III.98
Sufi -, V.24
- of ego, XIII.174-192
- of youth, III.103-13
Tranquility
IV.160
XIII.85-6
Transitory
IX.106
Treatment
good and bad -, III.241
Tree(s)
V.137
VI.108
IX.239
XI.61, 63, 236
- of wishes, XIII.111-13
Treta Yug
X.223
Triangle
XIII.101-2
Trimurti
II.37
IX.155, 206
XI.49
XIII.52, 101
Trinity
I.163
II.37, 186
V.13
VII.25
IX.103, 143, 155, 206
XI.50

XIII.52, 102
Trishul
XIII.93
Trisula
IX.214
Trust
I.44, 48, 95
II.223
VI.163
VII.87, 95
VIII.115, 245
IX.35, 57, 194
X.79
XII.100
Truth
I.20, 45, 56, 145-6, 185, 189, 198-9, 201-2, 240
II.64, 78, 164, 181, 185
III.204
IV.207, 214, 275
V.15-6
VI.22, 136, 193, 209, 266-7
VII.239
VIII.21, 200, 287, 303, 306
IX.17, 32, 49, 65, 77, 81, 88, 89, 90-1, 103, 107, 137, 142, 164, 182, 195, 200, 208, 213, 224, 227, 236-8, 240, 246-8, 260, 262, 265-7, 271, 279
X.23-6, 50, 105
XI.164, 190, 220, 227, 230, 237, 242, 246-9, 251, 254-5, 258-9
XIII.12
absolute -, XI.236
beauty of -, XIII.92
divine -, IX.247
knower of -, IX.224
message of -, IX.190
religious -, IX.118
seeking for -, IX.56
struggle for -, VIII.326-7
- and beauty, VII.19
- and illusion, X.26
- and the cross, VIII.184, 189
- beneath religions, XII.12
- is simple, XI.18
- vs. facts, VIII.133; XI.100
Tsar
XIII.17
Tuesday
XIII.42
Tulsidas
VI.87
Tumbara
II.115
X.227
Tuning
I.137, 179-81
IX.146
- of heart, VIII.271-87
- of spirit, XI.205-9
- to infinite, VI.74
Turban(s)
IX.214
Turkey
IV.164
Twins
VIII.92
Tyrrany
IX.85

Ugliness
XI.77, 238
Ummi
IX.150
Una (play)
XII.215-31
Unbelief
IX.57, 76
Unbeliever(s)
IX.138, 226
XI.228
Understanding
I.149
II.245
III.92
VI.89
VII.158, 256
VIII.106, 270, 292
IX.37, 200, 214
X.21-2, 32-3
XI.231, 238

desire for -, VII.158
- and vibration, XI.24
Unfoldment
I.232
IX.129
- of the soul, VIII.288-97
Unfulfillment
I.172
Unhappiness
I.150
VI.11
source of -, VII.181
Unification
IX.272
Uniformity
II.100
IX.11-14, 22
XII.56
unity and -, IX.11-4
Union
II.60, 133
IV.125
V.182, 202
VII.139
VIII.15
IX.11, 13, 35
sacred -, III.154
- with God, I.19, 21
United States
III.128
Unity
I.18, 33, 87, 237
II.97, 124, 151
VII.139
VIII.97, 130, 135, 172
IX.11-14, 79, 144, 222, 249, 256, 258, 263, 267, 270-3
XI.44, 254
- and uniformity, IX.11-4
- of people, IX.13
- *of Religious Ideals* (book), IX
realization of -, IX.12
spirit of -, IX.14
Universal Worship
IX.270-9
X.254
Universe
V.30, 61
IX.206-7, 222
XI.243
key to mystery of -, IX.119
- in man, XII.47-51
Unknown
dependence upon the VII.245-6
- dimension, XIII.160-1
Unlearning
I.93, 162
II.160
IV.108-12, 124
VI.219, 273-4
Unlettered
IX.150
Unnatural
XI.185
Unseen
I.20
seen and -, V.213-4
Unworthiness
XI.140
Upanishads
X.130
Upsaras
V.54
VII.137, 243
X.222
Urdu-Hindustani
X.217
Uruj
I.30
V.14, 60
Usman Haruni
IX.235-6

Vaccination
- and inoculation, VIII.249-50
Vacuum
XI.22, 53, 60-1, 63
Vadan
VII.239, 256, 267
XI.169
Vahm (imagination)
IV.48
Vak (Goddess of Speech)

VIII.204
Vairagi(s)
II.64
XII.108, 116
Vairagya
I.99-101
VI.57
IX.219
X.94, 234, 241
XIII.81-2, 126
Vaishas
V.125
IX.156
Vaishnavas
XIII.114-5
Valmiki
II.115
IX.158
X.233
Value
III.254
VI.103, 157
VII.268
changes in -s, X.92
real -s, III.171
-s, VIII.291
Vanaprasti
V.121
Vanavasa
IX.159
Vanity
III.220, 238
V.250
IX.127
XI.245
XIII.178-9, 188-9
Variety
I.237
III.131
IX.79, 144
XI.22, 254
Vashista
IX.158
Vedanta
II.90
V.13
VI.28
VII.52, 126
VIII.18, 19, 37, 46, 163, 189, 206
IX.183, 257
X.222, 241
XI.217
XII.94, 96
XIII.53, 86
Vedantists
IX.201
Vedas
X.214, 259
XIII.95
Vegetable
- kingdom, I.28, 90, 111, 135
- quality, XI.155-6
-s, XI.27
Vegetarianism
XIII.213-215
Veil
III.140
VIII.320
IX.222, 225, 260
Veneration
IX.204
Venus
- of Milo, III.161
Vibration(s)
I.152, 209
II.13, 17-22, 37, 57, 85, 91, 106-8, 118, 123, 128, 131, 141, 160, 170, 185, 202, 209, 213, 230
IV.34
V.26, 28, 30,
VIII.145, 156
IX.222
X.222
XI.22, 25-34, 58, 105, 249
XII.60, 118
XIII.294
degree of -, XI.26
electric -, IV.89
law of -, I.11, 137; XI.25, 27
rate of -, XI.29
speed of -, XI.23-5, 27
Vice
IX.209
Victory

III.262
IX.159, 195, 240
final -, III.262
Vignamayakosh
XIII.127
Vijnanamaya akasha
IX.219-20
Vilayat
XII.77
Vina
II.56, 75, 103-5, 136
Sarasvati -, II.104
Viprit Karnai
XIII.72-3
Virgins
V.34
ten -, IX.226-7; XIII.130-1
wise and foolish -, XIII.130
Virtue
I.23
III.44
V.158
VI.124
VIII.76, 79, 99, 233, 281, 322
IX.39, 67, 178, 187, 236, 244
XI.188, 236, 244
XIII.271
greatest human -, IX.119
ideas of -, VII.198
necessary -, IX.115
real -, XI.118
- and sin, VII.132; VIII.99
- of not judging, VIII.109
- of pirates, VIII.199
-s, I.59, 122
Vishnu
I.193
IX.147, 206
X.42, 188
XI.49
XIII.285
Vision(s)
I.39, 168
II.257
III.228
IV.149, 213, 227
VI.130
VIII.194
X.189
XII.66
clear -, IV.263
divine -, IX.67-8
- of God, IX.256
- *of God and Man* (book)II-124
- of mystic, XI.210-14
Vitality
I.26
XI.30
Viwadi
II.54
Vocation
I.26
VI.16-7
Voice
II.55, 110, 113, 115-20, 131, 135, 145, 159, 173, 180, 201, 205, 209, 212, 216
IV.207
VII.106
XI.89-91
elements of -, II.116
inner -, IX.149
jelal -, II.115
jemal -, II.115
kemal -, II.115
power of-, XIII.157
singing -, II.119
speaking -, II.117
- of God, IX.243
-s, II.201-8
Voltaire
XI.147
Vow
I.50
Vowels
II.34, 170
- and consonants, XII.120

Wadi
II.54
Wafah
XIII.194
Wagner

I. 253
II.136, 161
VI.128
IX.180
X.231, 25
Wahdaniat
I.111
II.67
V.25
Wahdat
I.111
II.67
V.17, 25, 33
Wajad
I.43
II.60, 67, 94
V.32
IX.115
X.139
Walayat
VII.208
Wali
I.29
V.25
VII.226
IX.128, 129, 132
XI.216
XII.146
Wanaprastha-shrama
VII.210
XII.110
War
I.138
III.197
IV.164
VI.77, 183
VII.166
IX.21, 87, 132, 162, 254
holy -, IX.21
no need for -, VII.196
-s, I.15; IX.119, 248
Warfare
IX.144, 161
Warning
IV.243
Warrior
IX.144
Water
I.112
IV.80
VIII.72, 266
IX.176, 188, 217-8
XIII.107, 161-2
magnetized -, IV.80-1
sound of -, II.15
symbol of -, XIII.106-7
- and man's heart, VIII.266-9
- and the loving quality, VIII.287
- element, X.161
Wazifa
II.64, 133
IV.250
VIII.63
IX.88
XIII.31
Weakness
II.177
IV.89
VI.100
VII.112-3
IX.209
XI.165
XIII.227-8
- and mastery, VII.160
Wealth
VI.147
VII.110
IX.112, 259
X.135
XI.257
XII.52-9
blindness of -, VII.173
spiritual -, XI.257
Weapons
sacred -, IX.207, 214
Wedding
- customs, XIII.39
Wednesday
XIII.43
Weight
VII.103
West
XIII.14, 17, 26
XI.47, 148
- and East, XII.56

Whole
study of the -, XIII.58-9
Why?
I.54, 145
IV.214
VIII.130
Wickedness
VI.170
XI.152
Will
V.44
IV.156-61, 169
VI.85, 168, 171, 223, 231
VIII.80-7, 225, 272, 278, 296
IX.107, 133, 192
XI.202
XII.84
conscious and unconscious -, VIII.143
destiny and free -, VIII.136-44
developing -power, VII.49, 62-4
divine -, VII.47, 57; IX.129-30
free -, III.209; V.218; VI.172, 231; VIII.136-44; XI.234
His -, IX.96
human and divine -, VII.46-51; IX.107-09; XIII.273-6
individual -, VIII.82-3, 143
personal -, IX.108
supreme -, IX.216
universal - (see also Kaza), VIII.82-3, 143
- as wish, VIII.80
- of God, I.157; VIII.71-2, 137, 143, 146, 244; IX.108-9, 134, 192; XI.229
- of infant, III.25
- of man and of God, VII.60
--power, I.183; II.234, 236; VI.85, 129; VII.57-64; VIII.50; XII.91; XI.101; XIII.258-60
--power in character building, III.197
-, wish and deaire, VIII.80-7
Wine
VI.141-4
VII.109
VIII.17, 122, 161
IX.110, 187-8, 201, 218
X.29, 124-5
XII.113
XIII.107-8
symbol of -, XIII.107
- as sacrament, XIII.213
- of selflessness, VIII.230
Wings
VIII.247
Wireless
XI.35
Wisdom
I.20, 38-9, 45, 67, 69, 75, 130, 134, 159
II.165
III.98, 108, 126
IV.108, 159
V.19-20, 56, 217
VI.53, 106
VII.50, 148
VIII.15, 71, 108, 244, 255, 292-3
IX.21, 33, 93, 104, 107, 111, 142-3, 160, 216, 226, 233, 252, 254, 257, 258, 260, 262-4, 266-7, 272, 275
XI.150, 180, 206, 211, 231-2, 235
XII.84
ancient -, IX.213
body of -, IX.219
culmination of -, VIII.111
divine -, I.134; VIII.13; IX.186, 257; XI.150-2
essence of -, XI.117
intellect and -, V.28; VII.233--8
perfect -, I.176
perfection of -, IX.49-50, 139, 141
plane of -, IX.220
prophets receive -, V.20
religion of -, IX.205
way of -, V.19
- and ignorance, V.217-8
- and intellect, VII.233-8

- a puzzle, XIII.109
Wise, the
VIII.292-3
IX.149, 180, 182, 203
XI.239
Wise Man
VI.242
X.30-1
XI.108, 149
-, spiritual and worldly, IX.30
Wish
I.172
IV.258
VIII.80-7
tree of -es, VIII.115; XIII.111-13
will, - and desire, VIII.80-7
-es, VIII.137
-es granted, VIII.129
Wit
XI.109
Witch
I.159
Woman, -en
III.122, 149
V.34
VII.265
XIII.23, 29
four types of -, III.135-7
rights of -, IX.31
seclusion of -, XIII.20-4
veiled Eastern -, III.139
Western -, III.139
- in East, III.158
- in Islam, III.159
Wonder(s)
II.28
V.65
VII.107
X.94
Word(s)
I.148
II.157, 162, 186, 190-1
III.222
IV.251
VI.250
VII.142, 243
VIII.154, 204, 209
IX.28, 216, 265
X.69, 207
XI.24, 32, 89-91, 115, 212, 240
XII.38, 118-24
divine -, IX.135
first was -, IX.223
intuitive -, II.173
lost -, II.174, 184
mystery of -, II.165, 168
origins of -, II.64
power of -, II.157, 162, 164-5, 167, 172, 179; XIII.78-9
Power of - (book), II.153-95
sacred -, I.152; IV.80; XI.91
secret of -, II. 181
suggestion by - and voice, XI.89-91
the -, XII.118-24
- and idea, XIII.75-6
- body of idea, XIII.75
- of the prophet, IX.138, 147, 151
-s, IV.205
- that was lost, II.184-8
Work
II.214
III.207, 246
IV.172
path is lifelong -, XII.101
subtle -, X.97
- of inner life, I.70
World
I.52
IV.233, 274
V.50
VII.55, 132
IX.36
X.34, 184, 241, 255
XI.55, 199
created -, IX.223
end of -, V.60-1
objective -, XI.192
outside -, influence of, IV.147
present need of -, X.255-7
seen -, XI.55
unseen -, XI.149; XI.55-6
- of angels, V.100-4

- of God, IX.239
--message, IX.241
- reconstruction, X.248-51
Worry
XI.258
Worship
I.20, 91
V.14-5, 203-4
VI.187
VII.22, 28
IX.37, 76, 120, 155, 166-7, 176, 197, 202-3, 265, 267, 274, 275, 278
X.129
XI.149
XIII.197
Brahmin symbolical form of -, IX.215-6
forms of Islamic -, IX.196-7
forms of -, in Hinduism, IX.155-6
Hindu symbolical form of -, XIII.113-16
ideal of -, IX.204
manner of -, VII.27
Universal -, IX.274-9
- in Islam, IX.197
- of God, IV.287
Worthiness
XI.140
Wrestler
IV.144
Wrong
X.52
right and -, III.250; VII.28-9
Wrongdoers
our dealings with -, III.250-1
Wujud
V.88, 143, 230

Yad-e-baiza
IV.77
Yag
IX.155
Yagna
IX.155
Yahuva
II.66
Yaqin
I.183, 204
X.100-1
Yashmak
XIII.21
Yawning
IV.74
Yearning
IX.75
Yeshoda
IX.160
Yesterday
-, today and tomorrow, X.172-4
-, *Today and Tomorrow* (book), X.155ff
Yima Jamshed
XIII.107
Yoga
I.143
II.92, 98, 103, 125, 180, 116, 143
VII.208
IX.91
X.45, 97, 154
XII.84, 105
-s, different, XII.103
Yogi(s)
I.143
IV.72, 193
VIII.15, 75
IX.257
X.45, 216
XI.45
XIII.21, 95-6, 151-2, 295
- on reincarnation, VIII.168
Youth
IV.282
XI.148, 154-5
attitudes of -, III.103
awakening of -, III.142-3
blindness of -, III.108-9
definition of -, III.75
disorders of -, III.109
early -, III.75
education of -, III.75-86

guidance of -, III.104, 106-7
imagination of -, III.77
impatience of -, III.106
memory of -, III.78
mind of -, III.76
passion of -, III.105-6
powers in -, III.108
religious education of -, III.76
spiritual side of -, III.111
training of -, III.103-13

Yusuf and Zuleikha
V.155-7

Zafah, Mount
VIII.13

Zafar, Emperor
III.129
IV.254

Zahir
V.214
VIII.121
XII.163

Zahur
Nur--, I.27

Zakat
IX.197

Zarathushtra
VI.233
IX.78, 150, 175-8, 186, 214
X.109, 129-30, 154

Zardash
II.13, 130
IX.214
XIII.92

Zat
I.111, 161-3
II.13, 130
V.14
IX.102-3, 196

Zebah
IX.201

Zeb-un-Nissa
II.133
III.140
IV.268

Zemzem
II.206

Zeval
I.30
V.60

Zikr (Zikar)
I.42
II.108, 170, 173
IV.84
VIII.63, 283
X.86
XII.150
XIII.19, 264

Zoroaster
(see also Zarathushtra)
II.65
IV.77
VII.132
IX.49, 78, 175
X.67, 129, 253
XII.133
"Look at the sun...", IX.49
- on sin and virtue, VII.132

Zoroastrianism
IX.176
X.253

Zoroastrian(s)
IX.120, 155, 176-7, 218, 258
- scriptures, IX.177

Zuhur
II.65

Zuleikha
V.155-7
X.12

Zunnar
IX.177

Appendix I

THE AIMS OF THE SUFI MOVEMENT

The Movement is based upon the Sufi Message brought to the Western world by Hazrat Inayat Khan in 1910.

In his studies as an initiate in one of the ancient Sufi orders, Inayat Khan recognised the basic love and wisdom through which humanity may realize the purpose of life. He saw these two principles as enshrined in the ideals of all religions. He held that by honouring all, and respecting their differences, a basis for mutual understanding could be reached which would not be possible by seeking to convert one to the views of another.

In pursuance of his vision he came to the West, and taught in Europe and America until 1926 when, shortly before his passing, he returned to India. He called his teaching the Sufi Message and to propagate it he founded a body called the International Sufi Movement. In the constitution are enshrined the following Sufi Thoughts:

1. There is one God, the Eternal, the Only Being; none else exists save He.
2. There is one Master, the Guiding Spirit of all souls, who constantly leads his followers towards the light.
3. There is one Holy Book, the sacred manuscript of nature, the only scripture which can enlighten the reader.
4. There is one Religion, the unswerving progress in the right direction towards the ideal, which fulfils the life's purpose of every soul.
5. There is one Law, the Law of Reciprocity, which can be observed by a selfless conscience together with a sense of awakened justice.
6. There is one Brotherhood, the human brotherhood, which unites the children of earth indiscriminately in the fatherhood of God.
7. There is one Moral Principle, the love which springs forth from self-denial, and blooms in deeds of beneficence.
8. There is one Object of Praise, the beauty which uplifts the heart of its worshipper through all aspects from the seen to the unseen.

9. There is one Truth, the true knowledge of our being within and without which is the essence of all wisdom.
10. There is one Path, the annihilation of the false ego in the real, which raises the mortal to immortality and in which resides all perfection.

The Movement has the following Objects:

1. To realize and spread the knowledge of unity, the religion of love and wisdom, so that the bias of faiths and beliefs may of itself fall away, the human heart may overflow with love, and all hatred caused by distinctions and differences may be rooted out.
2. To discover the light and power latent in man, the secret of all religion, the power of mysticism, and the essence of philosophy, without interfering with customs or belief.
3. To help to bring the world's two opposite poles, East and West, closer together by the interchange of thought and ideals, that the Universal Brotherhood may form of itself, and man may meet with man beyond the narrow national and racial boundaries.

Regarding the aims of the Movement, we quote as follows from the words of Inayat Khan:

"The purpose of the Sufi Movement is to work towards unity. Its main object is to bring humanity, divided as it is into so many different sections, closer together in the deeper understanding of life. It is a preparation for a world service, chiefly in three ways. One way is the philosophical understanding of life; another is bringing about brotherhood among races, nations, and creeds; and the third way is the meeting of the world's greatest need, which is the religion of the day. Its work is to bring to the world that natural religion which has always been the religion of humanity: to respect one another's belief, scripture, and teacher. The Sufi message is the echo of the same divine message which has always come and will always come to enlighten humanity. It is not a new religion; it is the same message which is being given to humanity. It is the continuation of the same ancient religion which has always existed and will always exist, a religion which belongs to all teachers and all the scriptures.

Sufism in itself is not a religion nor even a cult with a distinct or definite doctrine. No better explanation of Sufism can be given than by saying that any person who has a knowledge of both outer and inner life is a Sufi. Thus there has never at any period of the world's history been a founder of Sufism, yet Sufism has existed at all times.

The present-day Sufi Movement is a movement of members of different nations and races united together in the ideal of wisdom; they believe that wisdom does not belong to any particular religion or race, but to the human race as a whole. It is a divine property which mankind has inherited; and it is in this realization that the Sufis, in spite of belonging to different nationalities, races, beliefs, and faiths, still unite and work for humanity in the ideal of wisdom.

The Sufi message warns humanity to get to know life better and to achieve freedom in life; it warns man to accomplish what he considers good, just, and desirable; it warns him before every action to note its consequences by studying the situation, his own attitude, and the method he should adopt.

Sufism not only guides those who are religious, mystical, or visionary, but the Sufi message gives to the world the religion of the day: and that is to make one's life a religion, to turn one's occupation or profession into a religion, to make one's ideal a religious ideal. The object of Sufism is the uniting of life and religion, which so far seem to have been kept apart. When a man goes to church once a week, and devotes all the other days of the week to his business, how can he benefit by religion? Therefore the teaching of Sufism is to transform everyday life into a religion, so that every action may bear some spiritual fruit.

The method of world reform which various institutions have adopted today is not the method of the Sufi Movement. Sufis believe that if evil is contagious, goodness must be even more so. The depth of every soul is good; every soul is searching for good, and by the effort of individuals who wish to do good in the world much can be done, even more than a materialistic institution can achieve. No doubt for the general good there are political and commercial problems to be solved; but that must not debar individuals from progress, for it is the individual progress through the spiritual path which alone can bring about the desired condition in the world.

The Sufi message is not for a particular race, nation, or church. It is a call to unite in wisdom. The Sufi Movement is a group of people belonging to different religions, who have not left their religions but who have learned to understand them better, and their love is the love for God and humanity instead of for a particular section of it. The principal work that the Sufi Movement has to accomplish is to bring about a better understanding between East and West, and between the nations and races of his world. And the note that the Sufi message is striking at the present time is the note which sounds the divinity of the human soul. If there is any moral principle that the Sufi Movement brings, it is this; that

the whole of humanity is like one body, and any organ of that body which is hurt or troubled can indirectly cause damage to the whole body. And as the health of the whole body depends upon the health of each part, so the health of the whole of humanity depends upon the health of every nation. Besides, to those who are awakening and feel that now is the moment to learn more of the deeper side of life, of truth, the Sufi Movement extends a helping hand without asking to what religion, sect, or dogma they belong. The knowledge of the Sufi is helpful to every person, not only in living his life rightly but in regard to his own religion. The Sufi Movement does not call a man away from his belief or chruch: it calls him to live it. In short, it is a movement intended by God to unite humanity in brotherhood and in wisdom."

From *The Sufi Message of Haztat Inayat Khan,* Volume IX

Appendix II

HAZRAT INAYAT KHAN MEMORIAL TRUST

THE Hazrat Inayat Khan Memorial Trust, located in New Delhi, has been created for religious and charitable purposes. It is founded on the Sufi Message of love, harmony and beauty, as brought by Hazrat Inayat Khan (1882-1927).

Its goal is twofold: It wants to unite all people longing for love, harmony and beauty; and it wants to create not only a physical opportunity for this to happen, but also to create the appropriate atmosphere.

Its original and first activity was—and remains to be—to take care of the Dargah (memorial tomb) of this Sufi saint and master, who has been working for human brotherhood, religious tolerance, mysticism in daily life, the unity of religious ideals and a practical life philosophy. Apart from his being an active and famous musician in the first decade of this century in India, he has been working mainly in the West, bringing about a greater understanding for the values, the philosophy and the music of India, thus preparing ground for later positive developments.

The Trust further undertakes, within the limits of its modest means, to render financial help to the needy, the destitute, for instance, by providing them with better housing and/or establish homes for them.

During the last ten years the Trust has succeeded to make the Dargah into a dignified place and to start making it suitable for the Sufi work. It is becoming a place of peace and happiness, for silence and meditation, a home for everybody looking for these experiences within or without, its atmosphere charging every open-hearted visitor with upliftment and new energy. It is intended to become an ecumenical meeting ground in the real sense of the word for Hindus, Buddhists, Parsis, Sikhs, Jains, Jews, Christians, Muslims, and all others with sympathy in their hearts. At the same time it must be a place for help to our fellow-men. Here everyone can feel at home and free, and can meet people from other circles on 'neutral' yet warm and inspired ground. It is a centre for the spreading of the ecumenical Sufi Message of love, harmony and beauty: a

Message of universal brotherhood and tolerance, a basis for inter-religious brotherhood, a platform for inter-communal understanding, a spiritual centre, and an 'akasha' for love, harmony and beauty.

Gradually, the land around the Dargah had become completely occupied by temporary dwellings of refugees and others. To enlarge the area for our direct use was a very difficult and expensive task, because the Trust wanted to help the tenants living on the spot in acquiring better accommodation, even with financial assistance to these tenants living in the very poor huts in this area. In other cases the Trust has given some help to a tenant in starting a business.

In this way it became also possible to make some space available for the social, medical and educative programmes of the Hope Project Charitable Trust, another Sufi organisation working in the name of Hazrat Inayat Khan. The work of this Trust is to provide free social services to those living in the community around the Dargah. It includes the Hazrat Inayat Khan Health Centre, where medical treatment and referral services are provided; two dispensaries are being run, one homeopathic, the other allopathic, which help about 250 patients a day. In the Milk programme milk is distributed every day to infants, pregnant mothers and the infirm. The Hazrat Inayat Khan Education Centre offers educational and vocational training for children and adults from the Basti; there is a school for women, girls and little boys for educational and vocational training, free of charge. The social work programme offers help to those who are in crisis situations, financial troubles, the disabled and anyone who is in need.

This is quite in the tradition of Sufi Dargahs in India: besides spiritual activities also the material requirements of those in need are provided for.

In 1988 the new Dargah building was inaugurated. It is constructed around the original mazaar (tomb) by ASEMA architects in close contact with the Trust. Its simple design in beautiful material and harmonious proportions may be a symbol for the scope each individual has for the design of his life and the development of his heart. With this new building new opportunities are opening up.

Even before that time the activities of the Trust have grown steadily, and have become more intense. During a greater part of the year there are daily prayers and meditations, weekly qawalli concerts, weekly classes of the Inner School; each month Universal Worship is held, where texts from the sacred scriptures of the major world religions are read; occasionally there are concerts of spiritual classical Indian music, music playing such an important role in Inayat Khan's Message; regularly

lectures and courses on modern Sufism are being given. On special occasions there is langar; the free distribution of food to the local population. There is a small library in a preliminary form, on the fields of Sufism, philosophy, psychology, mysticism and (comparative) religion.

Further new activities are being envisaged. The first of these is realised by the publication of this series of volumes on the Sufi Message by Hazrat Inayat Khan. In the near future the Trust may publish a Sufi journal: "The Alchemy of Happiness". Brotherhood meetings will be organised amongst followers of different religions in order to increase mutual tolerance through understanding and realisation of the essentials we have in common. Courses will be developed on the Sufi Message on subjects such as: the unity of religious ideals, moral culture as the way to God, the development of personality, the tuning of mind, heart and spirit, etc. Further opportunities will be created to participate in meditation, silence, prayer, and spiritual music in order to develop the feeling of sympathy within so that it may radiate. Staging concerts of spiritual classical Indian music will be continued, following the tradition of the great musician, Hazrat Inayat Khan has been. The library may develop into a scholarly one. In close contact with the Hope Charitable Trust further facilities will be offered in the field of social and welfare programmes.

In 1987 the Circle of Friends of Hazrat Sufi Inayat Khan was inaugurated. It is open to all those sympathising with the Sufi Message of today, who feel stirred by the ideas and ideals of love, harmony and beauty, balance and tolerance, understanding and moral culture; those who look for spiritual development yet standing in the world; who want to strengthen the unity of religious ideals; to all those, therefore, who want to unite with other friends in order to share and to contribute to the development of these ideals within onself, amongst one another, and around, on a foundation of ever growing sympathy.

For further information on the work of the Trust or on its Circle of Friends
apply to
Hazrat Inayat Khan Memorial Trust
129, Basti Hazrat Nizamuddin Aulia
(opposite Lodhi Hotel)
New Delhi-110013
Tel. 625833.

libraries and centres for modern Sufism. The foundation stone [illegible] [illegible] there is [illegible] [illegible] of [illegible] [illegible] population. There is [illegible] science, philosophy, psychology, [illegible] and [illegible]. Further new [illegible] [illegible] [illegible] [illegible] [illegible] [illegible] the [illegible] the development of personality [illegible] spiritual [illegible] opportunities will be created to practise meditation, dance, prayer and spiritual music in order to [illegible] will be offered to the field of [illegible] [illegible] [illegible].

In 1982 the Khanqah of Friends of Hazrat Sufi Inayat Khan was inaugurated. It is open to all those sympathising with the Sufi Message today who feel attracted by the ideas and ideals of love, harmony and beauty, balance and tolerance, understanding and mutual enrichment, who look for a global development, understanding in the world, who want to experience the unity of religious ideals. All those, in short, who want to unite with other friends towards [illegible] and to contribute to the development of these ideals which cannot be imposed but must stand on a foundation of ever-growing sympathy.

For further information on the work of the Dargah or its Circle of Friends apply to:

Hazrat Inayat Khan Memorial Trust
129, Basti Hazrat Nizamuddin Aulia
(opposite [illegible])
New Delhi-110013
Tel. [illegible]

Appendix III

ABOUT THE SERIES

Volume I. *The Way of Illumination*
The traditional Sufic outlook on life's values and purpose is re-expressed by Hazrat Inayat Khan in universal and contemporary concepts. Included are: *The Way of Illumination; The Inner Life; The Soul; Whence and Whither* and *The Purpose of Life*.

Volume II. *The Mysticism of Music, Sound and Word.*
Sufism traditionally used music as a means of transmitting the essence of mystical insight. Hazrat Inayat Khan integrates this concept of music with elements like sound and silence, vibration and the word, thoughts and inspiration, creating new dimensions for our lives, and thereby recomposing a musical concept extending beyond the tradition of time and culture.

Volume III. *The Art of Personality*
This volume contains the substances of Hazrat Inayat Khan's teaching on our Divine heritage and human relationships, including the science of life's forces. He suggests that the art of personality is the completion of nature and the culmination of heredity. Development of the personality is taken from before birth to the deepest aspects of consciousness.
Included are: *Education; Rasa Shastra; Character-Building and the Art of Personality; Moral Culture.*

Volume IV. *Mental Purification and Healing.*
In this volume the Sufi principles are explained concerning the influence the mind may exert on the body, in relation to the spiritual power within us, and concerning the possibilities of spiritual healing in conjunction with modern science.
Included are: *Health; Mental Purification; The Mind World.*

Volume V. *Spiritual Liberty.*
This volume contains a wealth of information about different aspects of Sufi mysticism.
Included are: *A Sufi Message of Spiritual Liberty: Aqibat: Life after Death; The Phenomenon of the Soul; Love, Human and Divine; Pearls from the Ocean Unseen.*

Volume VI. *The Alchemy of Happiness.*
Hazrat Inayat Khan always insisted that spiritual or mystical aspirations are of no avail if one's life is not lived as it should be. Under this title, forty lectures are collected that deal with life in all its aspects.

Volume VII. *In an Eastern Rose Garden.*
Talks given by Hazrat Inayat Khan on a variety of subjects. His ability to communicate the unity and relativity of his viewpoint on diverse subjects illustrates the essence of his mystical perception of life.

Volume VIII. *Sufi Teachings.*
A collection of talks on various practical and esoteric aspects of traditional Sufi teachings developed by Hazrat Inayat Khan in a modern and universal context.

Volume IX. *The Unity of Religious Ideals*
A systematically arranged collection of Hazrat Inayat Khan's addresses on what is perhaps the most important part of his teaching: the underlying unity of all religious thought and experience.

Volume X. *Sufi Mysticism*
Hazrat Inayat Khan situates the traditional concepts of initiation, discipleship, spiritual teaching and other esoteric aspects of Sufism in today's world. Besides the main part consisting of: *Sufi Mysticism* and *The Path of Initiation and Discipleship,* these subjects are included: *Sufi Poetry; Art: Yesterday, Today and Tomorrow; The Problem of the Day.*

Volume XI. *Philosophy, Psychology, Mysticism*
These later talks by Hazrat Inayat Khan, given during the last two years before his death, contain a clear overview of these topics in terms of his Sufic vision. This series of lectures may be considered his *magnum opus.* The Aphorisms at the end are sayings noted down by his pupils which Hazrat Inayat Khan expressed at different times and places to soothe or clarify the seeker.

Volume XII. *The Divinity of the Human Soul.*
The first part of this volume deals with the relationship of man and God. The second part is autobiographical. The third part contains four short plays written by Hazrat Inayat Khan for his pupils.
Included are: *The Vision of God and Man; Confessions; Four Plays.*

Volume XIII. *Sacred Readings: The Gatha's*
This volume contains the teachings derived from classes given by Hazrat Inayat Khan to his pupils at the earlier stages of their training.

Volume XIV. *Index to Volumes I-XIII.*
This volume is published for the first time. It will be of great interest for the student of Sufism.

Sufi Hazrat Inayat Khan was born in Baroda on July 5th, 1882. His father, Mashaik Rahmat Khan, was descended from Pir Jammashah. His mother, Begum Khadija, came from a Zamindar family of Mysore. He studied music at the Gayan Shala musical academy in Baroda (founded by his grandfather, Maula Bhaksh, court musician of the Maharaja of Baroda). He travelled throughout India and became very well known as a court singer and Saraswati Veena player. He was initiated in the Chishtia and Qadria Sufi Orders by Syed Abu Hashim Madani of Hyderabad and in his travels he studied the religious and mystical Orders of India.

At the age of 28, he left for the West with his brothers Mahboob Khan, Ali Khan and Musharaff Khan. Between 1910 and the twenties they performed music in the great concert halls of Europe and America, being the first professional group to present both Hindustani and Karnatic music to the West. Hazrat Inayat Khan, later succeeded by his brothers, founded the Sufi Movement. He delivered the Sufi Message of Love, Harmony and Beauty, amongst others through lectures which now are being published in India for the first time. He passed away on February 5th, 1927 in New Delhi.

Those desiring particulars regarding the activities in all countries of the Sufi Movement founded by Hazrat Inayat Khan should apply to the International Headquarters of the Movement as follows:

(for activities in India)	(for activities outside India)
Sufi Movement India, Dargah Hzt. Inayat Khan 129, Basti Hzt. Nizamuddin New Delhi-110013	General Secretariat, Sufi Movement, Anna Paulownastraat 78 2518 BJ The Hague Holland